THE COMPLETE
UTEN DIGITAL
AIR FRYER OVEN
COOKBOOK UK
WITH PICTURES

Simple, Fast and Delicious Air Fry, Bake, Crisp, Roast and More Recipes for Anyone to Cook with Uten Digital (Colour Edition)

Avery Parker

Table of Contents

INTRODUCTION

As an experienced cook, I've had the pleasure of experimenting with a wide range of kitchen appliances, but few have impressed me as much as the Uten Digital Air Fryer Oven. In this cookbook, I want to share with you the incredible potential and versatility of this innovative kitchen tool.

The Uten Digital Air Fryer Oven is not your average kitchen gadget; it's a culinary game-changer. With its sleek design and advanced technology, it redefines the way we approach cooking. Here are some of its standout features that have captured my culinary heart:

1. Multi-Functionality: This appliance is a true kitchen workhorse. It offers a staggering 12 cooking modes, including frying, baking, roasting vegetables, pork ribs, cupcakes, toasting, pizza, and more. Whatever your culinary aspirations may be, this air fryer oven has a mode to suit your needs.

2. Precision Cooking: What sets the Uten Digital Air Fryer Oven apart is its ability to cook with precision. The combination of the hot air circulation system and precise temperature and time settings ensures that your dishes come out evenly cooked, with a delightful contrast of crispy exteriors and juicy, tender interiors.

3. User-Friendly Interface: The clear LCD display and touch screen controls make it incredibly easy to navigate through the various cooking options. Plus, you have the flexibility to manually adjust the temperature and cooking time to fine-tune your culinary creations.

4. Safety First: Safety is paramount, and this appliance doesn't disappoint. It features a circuit protection system that ensures safe operation, automatically entering standby mode if the temperature exceeds a certain limit.

5. Ample Capacity: With a generous 10-liter capacity, it's capable of preparing dishes for a crowd. So whether you're cooking for your family or hosting a dinner party, this air fryer oven has you covered.

6. Wide Temperature Range: It offers an extensive temperature control range, making it suitable for everything from defrosting at 25-60°C to cooking at temperatures between 80-200°C. This versatility ensures that it can handle a wide array of recipes.

7. Thoughtful Design: The Uten Digital Air Fryer Oven has been designed with the user in mind. Features like built-in lighting for easy monitoring, a countdown timer with automatic shutoff, and a removable double-layer heat-resistant tempered glass door for heat retention all contribute to its overall user-friendliness.

8. Whisper-Quiet Operation: Unlike many traditional air fryers that can be noisy, this product boasts a new air duct design and fan blades that significantly reduce noise, ensuring a peaceful cooking experience that won't disrupt your home life.

In writing this cookbook, my goal is to help you unlock the full potential of the Uten Digital Air Fryer Oven. Together, we'll explore a wide range of recipes and cooking techniques, from breakfast delights to gourmet dinners and even delectable desserts. So, let's embark on this culinary journey and discover the endless possibilities that await in your kitchen with the Uten Digital Air Fryer Oven.

Exploring the Benefits of Cooking with an Air Fryer Oven

Cooking with an air fryer oven, such as the Uten Digital Air Fryer Oven, opens up a world of culinary possibilities while offering numerous benefits that can enhance your cooking experience. Let's delve into some of these advantages and explore how this appliance can revolutionize your approach to meal preparation.

- **Healthier Cooking:** One of the foremost advantages of using an air fryer oven is its ability to promote healthier cooking. Here's how:

- **Less Oil, Less Fat:** Traditional frying methods often require copious amounts of oil, resulting in dishes that are loaded with unhealthy fats. With an air fryer oven, you can achieve that coveted crispy texture with only a fraction of the oil, significantly reducing the calorie and fat content of your meals.

- **Preservation of Nutrients:** The hot air circulation system in the air fryer oven ensures that your food cooks evenly at lower temperatures, which helps to preserve the natural vitamins and minerals present in your ingredients. This means you can enjoy the nutritional benefits of your favourite foods without sacrificing taste.

- **Faster Cooking Times:** Air fryer ovens typically cook food faster than conventional ovens. This is due to the rapid and even distribution of heat, allowing you to prepare meals in less time.

- **Energy Efficiency:** Using an air fryer oven requires less energy compared to heating a full-sized oven. This not only saves on your electricity bill but also contributes to a more eco-friendly kitchen.

Cooking with the Uten Digital Air Fryer Oven is a transformative experience that offers healthier cooking, increased efficiency, and unparalleled versatility. Say goodbye to excessive oil and long cooking times, and embrace a more convenient and nutritious way of preparing your favourite dishes. This appliance has the power to replace traditional cooking methods, making it a must-have addition to your kitchen arsenal.

CHAPTER 1
BREAKFAST DELIGHTS

Simple Breakfast Frittata

| PREP TIME: 15 minutes
| COOK TIME: 20 minutes

cooking spray.
4 eggs, lightly beaten
115 g breakfast sausage, fully cooked and crumbled
55 g cheddar cheese, shredded
1 green onion, chopped
2 tbsps. red bell pepper, diced
1 pinch cayenne pepper

1. Grease a non-stick 15x5-cm cake pan with cooking spray.
2. Whisk together eggs with sausage, green onion, bell pepper, chedda cheese and cayenne in a bowl.
3. Transfer the egg mixture in the greased cake pan.
4. Insert the drip tray into the bottom of the unit.
5. Arrange the cake pan on the air rack. Place air rack into unit by sliding through the side grooves and onto the back lip.
6. Press the On/Off button, select Bake setting, set the temperature to 185ºC and the cooking time to 20 minutes. Press the On/Off button again to begin cooking.
7. When the cooking is complete, remove the cake pan and serve warm.

Crispy Streaky Rashers

| PREP TIME: 1 minutes
| COOK TIME: 12 minutes

½ tbsp. olive oil
6 streaky rashers

1. Grease the streaky rashers with olive oil and place on the rotating mesh basket.
2. Insert the drip tray into the bottom of the unit.
3. Secure the rotating mesh basket on the unit. Press the On/Off button, select Fries setting, set the temperature to 175ºC and the cooking time to 12 minutes. Select rotate function and press the On/Off button again to begin cooking, until crispy.
4. When the cooking is complete, transfer the streaky rashers and serve warm.

Healthy Blueberry Muffin

| PREP TIME: 5 minutes
| COOK TIME: 15 minutes

115 g blanched finely ground almond flour
2 large eggs, whisked
45 g fresh blueberries, chopped
10 g granulated sweetener
4 tbsps. salted butter, melted
2 tsps. baking powder

1. In a large bowl, add all the ingredients and combine well. Evenly pour the batter into six silicone muffin cups greased with cooking spray.
2. Insert the drip tray into the bottom of the unit.
3. Arrange the muffin cups on the air rack. Place air rack into unit by sliding through the side grooves and onto the back lip.
4. Press the On/Off button, select Cupcake setting, set the temperature to 160°C and the cooking time to 15 minutes. Press the On/Off button again to begin cooking, until the muffins are golden brown.
5. When the cooking is complete, let the muffins cool for 15 minutes to avoid crumbling. Serve warm.

Courgette Fritters

| PREP TIME: 15 minutes
| COOK TIME: 7 minutes

cooking spray
300 g courgette, grated and squeezed
200 g Halloumi cheese
2 eggs
35 g plain flour
1 tsp. fresh dill, minced
Salt and black pepper, to taste

1. Mix together all the ingredients in a large bowl.
2. Shape this mixture into small fritters.
3. Insert the drip tray into the bottom of the unit.
4. Spray the fritters with cooking spray and place on the air rack. Place air rack into unit by sliding through the side grooves and onto the back lip.
5. Press the On/Off button, set the temperature to 180°C and the cooking time to 7 minutes. Press the On/Off button again to begin cooking.
6. When the cooking is complete, transfer the fritters to a plate and serve warm.

Cinnamon Rolls

| PREP TIME: 10 minutes
| COOK TIME: 12 minutes

215 g shredded Mozzarella cheese
95 g blanched finely ground almond flour
60 g cream cheese, softened
10 g sweetener
1 tbsp. ground cinnamon
½ tsp. vanilla extract

1. In a large microwave-safe bowl, combine the Mozzarella cheese, cream cheese, and flour. Microwave the mixture on high for 90 seconds until the cheese is melted.
2. Add the vanilla extract and sweetener, and mix for 2 minutes until a dough forms.
3. Once the dough is cool enough to work with your hands, for about 2 minutes, spread it out into a 24-cm× 8-cm rectangle on ungreased parchment paper. Evenly sprinkle the dough with cinnamon.
4. Starting at the long side of the dough, roll lengthwise to form a log. Slice the log into twelve even pieces.
5. Insert the drip tray into the bottom of the unit.
6. Spray the rolls with cooking spray and divide between the air racks. Place air racks into unit by sliding through the side grooves and onto the back lip.
7. Press the On/Off button, select Bake setting, set the temperature to 190ºC and the cooking time to 12 minutes. Press the On/Off button again to begin cooking. Cinnamon rolls will be done when golden around the edges and mostly firm.
8. When the cooking is complete, let the rolls to cool for 10 minutes and serve warm.

Mini Tomato Quiche

| PREP TIME: 15 minutes
| COOK TIME: 30 minutes

cooking spray
4 eggs
120 ml milk
115 g Gouda cheese, shredded
100 g tomatoes, chopped
30 g onion, chopped
Salt, to taste

1. Grease a large ramekin with cooking spray.
2. Mix together all the ingredients in the greased ramekin.
3. Insert the drip tray into the bottom of the unit.
4. Arrange the ramekin on the air rack. Place air rack into unit by sliding through the side grooves and onto the back lip.
5. Press the On/Off button, select Bake setting, set the temperature to 170ºC and the cooking time to 30 minutes. Press the On/Off button again to begin cooking.
6. When the cooking is complete, transfer the ramekin and serve warm.

Chicken Omelette

| PREP TIME: 15 minutes
| COOK TIME: 16 minutes

cooking spray
1 tsp. butter
3 eggs
1 onion, chopped
50 g chicken, cooked and shredded
½ jalapeño pepper, seeded and chopped
Salt and black pepper, to taste

1. Grease an 15x5-cm cake pan with cooking spray.
2. Heat the butter in a frying pan over medium heat and add the chopped onions.
3. Sauté for about 5 minutes and add the jalapeño pepper.
4. Sauté for about 1 minute and stir in the chicken.
5. Turn off the heat and keep aside.
6. Meanwhile, whisk together the eggs, salt, and black pepper in a bowl.
7. Place the chicken mixture into the prepared cake pan and top with the egg mixture.
8. Insert the drip tray into the bottom of the unit.
9. Arrange the cake pan on the air rack. Place air rack into unit by sliding through the side grooves and onto the back lip.
10. Press the On/Off button, select Bake setting, set the temperature to 180ºC and the cooking time to 10 minutes. Press the On/Off button again to begin cooking.
11. When the cooking is complete, remove the cake pan and serve hot.

Puffed Egg Tarts

| PREP TIME: 10 minutes
| COOK TIME: 24 minutes

15 ml olive oil
1 sheet frozen puff pastry half, thawed and cut into 4 squares
4 large eggs
85 g Cheddar cheese, shredded and divided
1 tbsp. fresh parsley, minced

1. Brush the pastry squares with olive oil.
2. Insert the drip tray into the bottom of the unit.
3. Arrange 2 pastry squares on each air rack. Place air racks into unit by sliding through the side grooves and onto the back lip.
4. Press the On/Off button, select Bake setting, set the temperature to 200ºC and the cooking time to 24 minutes. Press the On/Off button again to begin cooking.
5. After 10 minutes, press the On/Off button, press each square gently with a metal tbsp. to form an indentation. Place 3 tbsps. of cheese in each hole and top with 1 egg each. Press the On/Off button to continue cooking.
6. When the cooking is complete, transfer the tarts to a plate and sprinkle with half the parsley. Serve warm.

Cauliflower Hash Brown

PREP TIME: 20 minutes **COOK TIME:** 10 minutes	Cooking spray 2 tsps. rapeseed oil 130 g cauliflower, finely grated, soaked and drained 2 tbsps. xanthan gum 2 tsps. chilli flakes 1 tsp. onion powder 1 tsp. garlic Salt, to taste Pepper powder, to taste

1. Heat the rapeseed oil in a non-stick pan and add the cauliflower.
2. Sauté for about 4 minutes and transfer the cauliflower into a plate.
3. Mix the cauliflower with xanthan gum, salt, chilli flakes, garlic and onion powder.
4. Combine well and refrigerate the hash for about 20 minutes.
5. Insert the drip tray into the bottom of the unit.
6. Spray the hash with cooking spray and arrange on the air rack. Place air rack into unit by sliding through the side grooves and onto the back lip.
7. Press the On/Off button, select Vegetable setting, set the temperature to 150ºC and the cooking time to 10 minutes. Press the On/Off button again to begin cooking, flipping once halfway through.
8. When the cooking is complete, transfer the hash to a plate and serve warm.

French Toast Sticks

PREP TIME: 10 minutes **COOK TIME:** 5 minutes	Cooking spray 4 bread, sliced into sticks 2 eggs, gently beaten 1 pinch nutmeg 1 pinch ground cloves 1 pinch cinnamon Salt, to taste

1. Whisk the eggs with salt, cinnamon, nutmeg and ground cloves in a small bowl.
2. Dip the bread sticks in the egg mixture.
3. Insert the drip tray into the bottom of the unit.
4. Spray the air rack with cooking spray and arrange the bread sticks on the air rack. Place air rack into unit by sliding through the side grooves and onto the back lip.
5. Press the On/Off button, select Bake setting, set the temperature to 185ºC and the cooking time to 5 minutes. Press the On/Off button again to begin cooking, flipping in between.
6. When the cooking is complete, transfer the sticks to a plate and serve warm.

CHAPTER 2

FISH AND SEAFOOD ESCAPADES

Quick Tiger Prawn

| PREP TIME: 10 minutes
| COOK TIME: 5 minutes

15 ml olive oil
230 g tiger prawns
½ tsp. old bay seasoning
¼ tsp. cayenne pepper
¼ tsp. smoked paprika
Salt, to taste

1. Mix all the ingredients in a large bowl until well combined.
2. Insert the drip tray into the bottom of the unit.
3. Arrange the prawns on the air rack. Place air rack into unit by sliding through the side grooves and onto the back lip.
4. Press the On/Off button, select Prawn setting, set the temperature to 200ºC and the cooking time to 5 minutes. Press the On/Off button again to begin cooking, flipping once in between.
5. When the cooking is complete, transfer the prawns to a plate and serve warm.

Sesame Seeds Coated Tuna

| PREP TIME: 15 minutes
| COOK TIME: 6 minutes

2 (170 g) tuna steaks
1 egg white
60 g white sesame seeds
15 g black sesame seeds
Salt and black pepper, as required

1. Whisk the egg white in a shallow bowl.
2. Mix the sesame seeds, salt, and black pepper in another bowl.
3. Dip the tuna steaks into the whisked egg white and dredge into the sesame seeds mixture.
4. Insert the drip tray into the bottom of the unit.
5. Spray the tuna steaks with cooking spray and arrange on the air rack. Place air rack into unit by sliding through the side grooves and onto the back lip.
6. Press the On/Off button, select Fish setting, set the temperature to 200ºC and the cooking time to 6 minutes. Press the On/Off button again to begin cooking, flipping once in between.
7. When the cooking is complete, transfer the tuna steaks onto serving plates and serve hot.

Buttered Scallops

| PREP TIME: 15 minutes
| COOK TIME: 4 minutes

cooking spray
15 g butter, melted
340 g sea scallops, cleaned and patted very dry
½ tbsp. fresh thyme, minced
Salt and black pepper, as required

1. Mix the sea scallops, butter, thyme, salt, and black pepper in a bowl.
2. Insert the drip tray into the bottom of the unit.
3. Spray the scallops with cooking spray and arrange on the air rack. Place air rack into unit by sliding through the side grooves and onto the back lip.
4. Press the On/Off button, select Fish setting, set the temperature to 200°C and the cooking time to 4 minutes. Press the On/Off button again to begin cooking, flipping halfway through.
5. When the cooking is complete, transfer the scallops in a platter and serve hot.

Cajun Spiced Salmon

| PREP TIME: 10 minutes
| COOK TIME: 8 minutes

cooking spray
2 (200 g) (2 cm thick) salmon fillets
1 tbsp. Cajun seasoning
15 ml fresh lemon juice
½ tsp. caster sugar

1. Season the salmon evenly with Cajun seasoning and sugar.
2. Insert the drip tray into the bottom of the unit.
3. Spray the salmon fillets with cooking spray and arrange on the air rack. Place air rack into unit by sliding through the side grooves and onto the back lip.
4. Press the On/Off button, select Fish setting, set the temperature to 185°C and the cooking time to 8 minutes. Press the On/Off button again to begin cooking, flipping halfway through.
5. When the cooking is complete, transfer the salmon fillets in the serving plates. Drizzle with the lemon juice and serve hot.

Homemade Fish Fingers

| PREP TIME: 15 minutes
| COOK TIME: 12 minutes

Cooking spray
4 fish fillets
2 eggs
190 g whole-wheat panko bread crumbs
66 g whole-wheat flour
½ tbsp. dried parsley flakes
1 tsp. seasoned salt

1. Cut the fish fillets lengthwise into "finger."
2. In a shallow bowl, combine the whole-wheat flour and seasoned salt.
3. In a small bowl, whisk the eggs with 1 tsp. of water.
4. In another shallow bowl, mix the panko bread crumbs and parsley flakes.
5. Coat each fish finger in the seasoned flour, then in the egg mixture, and dredge them in the panko bread crumbs.
6. Spray the fish fingers with cooking spray and place on the rotating mesh basket.
7. Insert the drip tray into the bottom of the unit.
8. Secure the rotating mesh basket on the unit. Press the On/Off button, select Fries setting, set the temperature to 200ºC and the cooking time to 12 minutes. Select rotate function and press the On/Off button again to begin cooking, until golden brown.
9. When the cooking is complete, transfer the fish fingers to a plate and serve warm.

Spicy Orange Prawn

| PREP TIME: 20 minutes
| COOK TIME: 12 minutes

Cooking spray
454 g medium prawns, peeled and deveined, with tails off
80 ml orange juice
3 tsps. minced garlic
1 tsp. Old Bay seasoning
¼ to ½ tsp. cayenne pepper

1. In a medium bowl, combine the orange juice, garlic, Old Bay seasoning, and cayenne pepper.
2. Dry the prawns with paper towels to remove excess water.
3. Add the prawns to the marinade and stir to coat well. Cover with clingfilm and place in the refrigerator for 30 minutes so the prawns can soak up the marinade.
4. Insert the drip tray into the bottom of the unit.
5. Spray the air rack lightly with cooking spray and arrange the prawns on the air rack. Place air rack into unit by sliding through the side grooves and onto the back lip.
6. Press the On/Off button, select Prawn setting, set the temperature to 200ºC and the cooking time to 12 minutes. Press the On/Off button again to begin cooking, shaking halfway through.
7. When the cooking is complete, transfer the prawns to a plate and serve warm.

Cod with Asparagus

SERVES 2

| PREP TIME: 15 minutes
| COOK TIME: 11 minutes

15 ml olive oil
2 (170 g) boneless cod fillets
1 bunch asparagus
23 ml fresh lemon juice
2 tbsps. fresh parsley, roughly chopped
2 tbsps. fresh dill, roughly chopped
1 tsp. dried basil
Salt and black pepper, to taste

1. Mix the lemon juice, oil, basil, salt, and black pepper in a small bowl.
2. Combine the cod and ¾ of the oil mixture in another bowl.
3. Coat the asparagus evenly with remaining oil mixture.
4. Insert the drip tray into the bottom of the unit.
5. Arrange the asparagus on the air rack. Place air rack into unit by sliding through the side grooves and onto the back lip.
6. Press the On/Off button, set the temperature to 200ºC and the cooking time to 11 minutes. Press the On/Off button again to begin cooking.
7. After 3 minutes, press the On/Off button, place the cod fillets on another air rack and insert into the unit. Press the On/Off button again to continue cooking.
8. When the cooking is complete, transfer the cod fillets and asparagus in serving plates. Serve warm.

Wasabi Crab Cakes

SERVES 6

| PREP TIME: 20 minutes
| COOK TIME: 12 minutes

cooking spray
200 g lump crab meat, drained
1 medium red bell pepper, finely chopped
1 celery rib, finely chopped
2 large egg whites
100 g panko breadcrumbs, divided
3 spring onions, finely chopped
3 tbsps. mayonnaise
¼ tsp. prepared wasabi
Salt, to taste

1. Mix the spring onions, red pepper, celery, 40 g of breadcrumbs, egg whites, mayonnaise, wasabi, and salt in a large bowl.
2. Fold in the crab meat gently and combine well.
3. Place the remaining breadcrumbs in another bowl.
4. Insert the drip tray into the bottom of the unit.
5. Shape this crab mixture into 2-cm thick patties and arrange on the air rack. Spray with cooking spray and place air rack into unit by sliding through the side grooves and onto the back lip.
6. Press the On/Off button, select Fish setting, set the temperature to 190ºC and the cooking time to 12 minutes. Press the On/Off button again to begin cooking, flipping once halfway through.
7. When the cooking is complete, transfer the patties to a plate and serve warm.

Garlic-Lemon Tilapia

| PREP TIME: 5 minutes
| COOK TIME: 13 minutes

cooking spray
1 tbsp. olive oil
4 (170-g) tilapia fillets
1 tbsp. lemon juice
1 tsp. minced garlic
½ tsp. chilli powder

1. In a large, shallow bowl, mix together the olive oil, lemon juice, garlic, and chilli powder to make a marinade. Place the tilapia fillets in the marinade bowl and coat evenly.
2. Insert the drip tray into the bottom of the unit.
3. Spray the air rack with cooking spray and arrange on the air rack, leaving space between each fillet. Place air rack into unit by sliding through the side grooves and onto the back lip.
4. Press the On/Off button, select Fish setting, set the temperature to 190ºC and the cooking time to 13 minutes. Press the On/Off button again to begin cooking, until the fish is cooked and flakes easily with a fork.
5. When the cooking is complete, transfer the fillets to a plate and serve warm.

Breaded Flounder

| PREP TIME: 15 minutes
| COOK TIME: 12 minutes

60 ml rapeseed oil
3 (170 g) flounder fillets
120 g dry breadcrumbs
1 egg
1 lemon, sliced

1. Whisk the egg in a shallow bowl and mix the breadcrumbs and rapeseed oil in another bowl.
2. Dip the flounder fillets into the whisked egg and coat with the breadcrumb mixture.
3. Insert the drip tray into the bottom of the unit.
4. Spray the flounder fillets with cooking spray and arrange on the air rack. Place air rack into unit by sliding through the side grooves and onto the back lip.
5. Press the On/Off button, select Fish setting, set the temperature to 180ºC and the cooking time to 12 minutes. Press the On/Off button again to begin cooking, flipping halfway through cooking.
6. When the cooking is complete, transfer the flounder fillets onto serving plates and garnish with the lemon slices to serve.

CHAPTER 3
VEGETARIAN AND VEGAN OPTIONS

Cheesy Brussels Sprouts

| PREP TIME: 15 minutes
| COOK TIME: 10 minutes

cooking spray
15 ml extra-virgin olive oil
450 g Brussels sprouts, trimmed and halved
30 g Parmesan cheese, shredded
30 g panko breadcrumbs
15 ml balsamic vinegar
Salt and black pepper, to taste

1. Mix the Brussels sprouts, vinegar, olive oil, salt, and black pepper in a bowl and toss to coat well.
2. Insert the drip tray into the bottom of the unit.
3. Spray the air rack with cooking spray and arrange the Brussels sprouts on the air rack. Place air rack into unit by sliding through the side grooves and onto the back lip.
4. Press the On/Off button, select Vegetable setting, set the temperature to 200ºC and the cooking time to 10 minutes. Press the On/Off button again to begin cooking.
5. After 5 minutes, press the On/Off button and sprinkle with breadcrumbs and cheese. Press the On/Off button to continue cooking.
6. When the cooking is complete, transfer the Brussels sprouts to a bowl and serve hot.

Roasted Carrots with Herbs

| PREP TIME: 15 minutes
| COOK TIME: 14 minutes

6 large carrots, peeled and sliced lengthwise
60 ml olive oil
½ tbsp. fresh oregano, chopped
½ tbsp. fresh parsley, chopped
Salt and black pepper, to taste
115 ml fat-free Italian dressing
Salt, to taste

1. Mix the carrot slices and olive oil in a large bowl and toss to coat well.
2. Insert the drip tray into the bottom of the unit.
3. Arrange the carrot slices on the air rack. Place air rack into unit by sliding through the side grooves and onto the back lip.
4. Press the On/Off button, select Vegetable setting, set the temperature to 180ºC and the cooking time to 14 minutes. Press the On/Off button again to begin cooking, flipping halfway through cooking.
5. With 2 minutes remaining, press the On/Off button, sprinkle with herbs, salt and black pepper. Press the On/Off button to continue cooking.
6. When the cooking is complete, transfer the carrots to a plate and serve hot.

Spiced Butternut Squash

| PREP TIME: 15 minutes
| COOK TIME: 20 minutes

cooking spray
15 ml olive oil
1 medium butternut squash, peeled, seeded and cut into chunk
15 g pine nuts
2 tbsps. fresh coriander, chopped
2 tsps. cumin seeds
1/8 tsp. garlic powder
1/8 tsp. chilli flakes, crushed
Salt and ground black pepper, as required

1. Mix the squash, spices and olive oil in a large bowl.
2. Insert the drip tray into the bottom of the unit.
3. Spray the air rack with cooking spray and arrange the butternut squash chunks on the air rack. Place air rack into unit by sliding through the side grooves and onto the back lip.
4. Press the On/Off button, select Vegetable setting, set the temperature to 190ºC and the cooking time to 20 minutes. Press the On/Off button again to begin cooking, shaking halfway through.
5. When the cooking is complete, transfer the butternut squash chunks onto serving plates and serve garnished with pine nuts and coriander.

Asparagus with Almonds

| PREP TIME: 15 minutes
| COOK TIME: 6 minutes

60 ml olive oil
450 g asparagus
30 ml balsamic vinegar
25 g almonds, sliced
Salt and black pepper, to taste

1. Mix the asparagus, olive oil, vinegar, salt, and black pepper in a bowl and toss to coat well.
2. Insert the drip tray into the bottom of the unit.
3. Arrange the asparagus on the air rack and sprinkle with the almond slices. Place air rack into unit by sliding through the side grooves and onto the back lip.
4. Press the On/Off button, select Vegetable setting, set the temperature to 200ºC and the cooking time to 6 minutes. Press the On/Off button again to begin cooking, shaking halfway through.
5. When the cooking is complete, transfer the asparagus and almonds to a plate and serve hot.

Basil Tomatoes

| PREP TIME: 10 minutes
| COOK TIME: 10 minutes

Olive oil cooking spray
1 tbsp. fresh basil, chopped
2 tomatoes, halved
Salt and black pepper, as required

1. Spray the tomato halves evenly with olive oil cooking spray and sprinkle with salt, black pepper and basil.
2. Insert the drip tray into the bottom of the unit.
3. Arrange the tomato halves on the air rack, cut sides up. Place air rack into unit by sliding through the side grooves and onto the back lip.
4. Press the On/Off button, select Vegetable setting, set the temperature to 160ºC and the cooking time to 10 minutes. Press the On/Off button again to begin cooking.
5. When the cooking is complete, transfer the tomatoes onto serving plates and serve warm.

Red Bell Peppers Cups

| PREP TIME: 10 minutes
| COOK TIME: 8 minutes

½ tbsp. olive oil
8 mini red bell peppers, tops and seeds removed
85 g feta cheese, crumbled
1 tsp. fresh parsley, chopped
Freshly ground black pepper, to taste

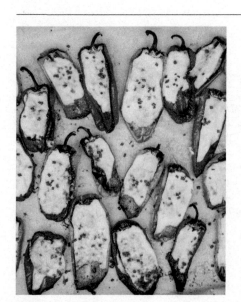

1. Mix the feta cheese, parsley, olive oil and black pepper in a bowl.
2. Stuff the red bell peppers with this feta cheese mixture.
3. Insert the drip tray into the bottom of the unit.
4. Spray the air rack with cooking spray and arrange the bell peppers on the air rack. Place air rack into unit by sliding through the side grooves and onto the back lip.
5. Press the On/Off button, select Vegetable setting, set the temperature to 200ºC and the cooking time to 8 minutes. Press the On/Off button again to begin cooking.
6. When the cooking is complete, transfer the bell peppers to a bowl and serve hot.

Hasselback Potatoes

| PREP TIME: 20 minutes
| COOK TIME: 30 minutes

60 ml olive oil
4 potatoes
15 g Parmesan cheese, shredded
1 tbsp. fresh chives, chopped

1. Cut slits along each potato about ½-cm apart with a sharp knife, making sure slices should stay connected at the bottom.
2. Insert the drip tray into the bottom of the unit.
3. Coat the potatoes with olive oil and arrange on the air rack. Place air rack into unit by sliding through the side grooves and onto the back lip.
4. Press the On/Off button, select Vegetable setting, set the temperature to 180ºC and the cooking time to 30 minutes. Press the On/Off button again to begin cooking.
5. When the cooking is complete, transfer the potatoes in a platter. Top with the chives and Parmesan cheese to serve.

Pesto Stuffed Mushrooms

SERVES 6

| PREP TIME: 10 minutes
| COOK TIME: 15 minutes

1 tbsp. olive oil
454 g baby Bella mushroom, stems removed
120 g nutritional yeast
80 g cashew, soaked overnight
60 g basil
2 cloves garlic
1 tbsp. lemon juice
Salt, to taste

1. In a food processor, blend the cashew nuts, nutritional yeast, basil, lemon juice, garlic and olive oil to combine well. Sprinkle with salt to taste.
2. Turn the mushrooms cap-side down and spread the pesto on the underside of each cap.
3. Insert the drip tray into the bottom of the unit.
4. Spray the air rack with cooking spray and arrange the mushrooms on the air rack. Place air rack into unit by sliding through the side grooves and onto the back lip.
5. Press the On/Off button, select Vegetable setting, set the temperature to 200ºC and the cooking time to 15 minutes. Press the On/Off button again to begin cooking.
6. When the cooking is complete, transfer the mushrooms to a plate and serve warm.

Spices Stuffed Aubergines

| PREP TIME: 15 minutes
| COOK TIME: 12 minutes

20 ml olive oil, divided
8 baby aubergines
¾ tbsp. dry mango powder
¾ tbsp. ground coriander
½ tsp. ground turmeric
½ tsp. ground cumin
½ tsp. garlic powder
Salt, to taste

1. Make 2 slits from the bottom of each aubergine leaving the stems intact.
2. Add 5 ml oil, mango powder, coriander, cumin, turmeric and garlic powder in a bowl and mix well.
3. Fill each slit of aubergines with this spices mixture. Brush the outside of each aubergine with remaining oil.
4. Insert the drip tray into the bottom of the unit.
5. Arrange the aubergines on the air rack. Place air rack into unit by sliding through the side grooves and onto the back lip.
6. Press the On/Off button, select Vegetable setting, set the temperature to 190ºC and the cooking time to 12 minutes. Press the On/Off button again to begin cooking.
7. When the cooking is complete, transfer the aubergines to a bowl and serve hot.

Courgette Balls

| PREP TIME: 5 minutes
| COOK TIME: 10 minutes

cooking spray
4 courgettes
1 egg
80 g grated coconut
47 g grated Parmesan cheese
1 tbsp. Italian herbs

1. Thinly grate the courgettes and dry with a cheesecloth, ensuring to remove all the moisture.
2. In a bowl, combine the courgettes with the egg, Parmesan, Italian herbs, and grated coconut, mixing well to incorporate everything. Using the hands, mould the mixture into balls.
3. Insert the drip tray into the bottom of the unit.
4. Spray the air rack with cooking spray and lay the courgette balls on the air rack. Place air rack into unit by sliding through the side grooves and onto the back lip.
5. Press the On/Off button, select Vegetable setting, set the temperature to 200ºC and the cooking time to 10 minutes. Press the On/Off button again to begin cooking, shaking halfway through.
6. When the cooking is complete, transfer the courgette balls to a plate and serve warm.

CHAPTER 4
BEEF BONANZA

Rosemary Beef Roast

SERVES 8

| PREP TIME: 5 minutes
| COOK TIME: 35 minutes

60 ml avocado oil
1 (900 g) top round beef roast, tied with kitchen string
2 tbsps. finely chopped fresh rosemary
2 tsps. minced garlic
Sea salt, Freshly ground black pepper, to taste

1. Season the beef roast generously with salt and pepper.
2. In a small bowl, whisk together the garlic, rosemary and avocado oil. Rub this mixture all over the roast. Cover loosely with aluminium foil or clingfilm and refrigerate for at least 12 hours or up to 2 days.
3. Remove the roast from the refrigerator and let sit at room temperature for about 1 hour.
4. Insert the drip tray into the bottom of the unit.
5. Slide the rotisserie rod through the center of the roast and secure the roast with the rotisserie forks. Secure the rotisserie spit in the unit.
6. Press the On/Off button, set the temperature to 160ºC and the cooking time to 35 minutes. Select rotate function and press the On/Off button again to begin cooking, until the meat is browned and an instant-read thermometer reads 50ºC at the thickest part (for medium-rare).
7. When the cooking is complete, transfer the meat to a cutting board, and let it rest for 15 minutes before thinly slicing and serving.

Beef Short Ribs

SERVES 8

| PREP TIME: 15 minutes
| COOK TIME: 12 minutes

cooking spray
1¾ kg bone-in beef short ribs
235 ml low-sodium soy sauce
115 ml rice vinegar
35 g spring onions, chopped
15 ml Sriracha
2 tbsps. brown sugar
1 tbsp. fresh ginger, finely grated
1 tsp. ground black pepper

1. Put the beef short ribs with all other ingredients in a resealable bag and seal the bag.
2. Shake to coat well and refrigerate overnight.
3. Insert the drip tray into the bottom of the unit.
4. Spray the air rack with cooking spray. Remove the short ribs from resealable bag and arrange on the air rack. Place air rack into unit by sliding through the side grooves and onto the back lip.
5. Press the On/Off button, select Ribs setting, set the temperature to 200ºC and the cooking time to 12 minutes. Press the On/Off button again to begin cooking, flipping once in between.
6. When the cooking is complete, transfer the ribs to a plate and serve hot.

Rib Eye Steak with Herbed Butter

SERVES 2

| PREP TIME: 20 minutes
| COOK TIME: 14 minutes

cooking spray
15 ml olive oil
2 (225 g) rib eye steaks
115 g unsalted butter, softened
2 tbsps. fresh parsley, chopped
2 tsps. garlic, minced
1 tsp. Worcestershire sauce
Salt and black pepper, to taste

1. Mix the butter, parsley, garlic, Worcestershire sauce, and salt in a bowl.
2. Arrange the butter mixture onto a greaseproof paper, roll into a log and refrigerate for about 3 hours.
3. Rub the steaks generously with olive oil, salt and black pepper.
4. Insert the drip tray into the bottom of the unit.
5. Spray the air rack with cooking spray and arrange the steaks on the air rack. Place air rack into unit by sliding through the side grooves and onto the back lip.
6. Press the On/Off button, select Steak setting, set the temperature to 200ºC and the cooking time to 14 minutes. Press the On/Off button again to begin cooking, flipping once in between.
7. When the cooking is complete, transfer the steaks onto serving plates and cut into desired size slices.
8. Cut the butter log into slices and top over the steaks to serve.

Simple Beef Steaks

SERVES 2

| PREP TIME: 5 minutes
| COOK TIME: 14 minutes

cooking spray
230 g quality cuts steaks
Salt and black pepper, to taste

1. Season the steaks evenly with salt and black pepper.
2. Insert the drip tray into the bottom of the unit.
3. Spray the steaks with cooking spray and arrange on the air rack. Place air rack into unit by sliding through the side grooves and onto the back lip.
4. Press the On/Off button, select Steak setting, set the temperature to 200ºC and the cooking time to 14 minutes. Press the On/Off button again to begin cooking, flipping halfway through.
5. When the cooking is complete, transfer the steaks to a plate and serve warm.

Classic Beef Burgers

| PREP TIME: 20 minutes
| COOK TIME: 10 minutes

cooking spray
450 g beef mince
4 whole-wheat hamburger buns, split and toasted
3-4 drops liquid smoke
15 ml Worcestershire sauce
1 tsp. Maggi seasoning sauce
1 tsp. dried parsley
½ tsp. onion powder
½ tsp. garlic powder
Salt and ground black pepper, as required

1. Mix the beef, sauces, liquid smoke, parsley, and spices in a medium bowl.
2. Shape this beef mixture into4 equal-sized patties.
3. Insert the drip tray into the bottom of the unit.
4. Spray the patties with cooking spray and arrange on the air rack. Place air rack into unit by sliding through the side grooves and onto the back lip.
5. Press the On/Off button, set the temperature to 175ºC and the cooking time to 10 minutes. Press the On/Off button again to begin cooking, flipping halfway through.
6. When the cooking is complete, transfer the patties to a plate and serve on a bun.

Buttered Striploin Steak

| PREP TIME: 10 minutes
| COOK TIME: 12 minutes

20 g butter, softened
2 (200 g) striploin steaks
Salt and black pepper, to taste

1. Rub the steaks generously with salt and black pepper and coat with butter.
2. Insert the drip tray into the bottom of the unit.
3. Arrange the steaks on the air rack. Place air rack into unit by sliding through the side grooves and onto the back lip.
4. Press the On/Off button, select Steak setting, set the temperature to 200ºC and the cooking time to 12 minutes. Press the On/Off button again to begin cooking, flipping once in between.
5. When the cooking is complete, transfer the steaks and cut into desired size slices to serve.

Beef and Veggie Kebabs

| PREP TIME: 20 minutes
| COOK TIME: 12 minutes

cooking spray
60 ml olive oil
450 g sirloin steak, cut into chunks
225 g baby Bella mushrooms, stems removed
1 red onion, cut into 2.5-cm pieces
1 large bell pepper, seeded and cut into 2.5-cm pieces
60 ml soy sauce
1 tbsp. garlic, minced
1 tsp. brown sugar
½ tsp. ground cumin
Salt and black pepper, to taste

1. Mix the soy sauce, olive oil, garlic, brown sugar, cumin, salt, and black pepper in a large bowl.
2. Coat the steak cubes generously with this marinade and refrigerate to marinate for about 30 minutes.
3. Thread the steak cubes, mushrooms, bell pepper, and onion onto metal skewers.
4. Insert the drip tray into the bottom of the unit.
5. Spray the skewers with cooking spray and arrange on the air rack. Place air rack into unit by sliding through the side grooves and onto the back lip.
6. Press the On/Off button, set the temperature to 200ºC and the cooking time to 12 minutes. Press the On/Off button again to begin cooking, flipping once in between.
7. When the cooking is complete, transfer the skewers in a platter and serve hot.

Spiced Beef Roast

| PREP TIME: 10 minutes
| COOK TIME: 50 minutes

60 ml olive oil
1 kg beef eye of round roast, trimmed
½ tsp. cayenne pepper
½ tsp. onion powder
½ tsp. garlic powder
½ tsp. ground black pepper
Salt, to taste

1. Rub the roast generously with all the spices and coat with olive oil.
2. Insert the drip tray into the bottom of the unit.
3. Slide the rotisserie rod through the center of the roast and secure the roast with the rotisserie forks. Secure the rotisserie spit in the unit.
4. Press the On/Off button, set the temperature to 180ºC and the cooking time to 50 minutes. Select rotate function and press the On/Off button again to begin cooking.
5. When the cooking is complete, transfer the roast to a plate and cover with foil. Cut into desired size slices and serve.

Beef and Mushroom Meatloaf

| PREP TIME: 15 minutes
| COOK TIME: 25 minutes

15 ml olive oil
450 g lean beef mince
1 egg, lightly beaten
2 mushrooms, thickly sliced
1 small onion, finely chopped
25 g dry breadcrumbs
Salt and ground black pepper, as required

1. Mix the olive oil, beef, onion, breadcrumbs, egg, salt, and black pepper in a bowl until well combined.
2. Shape the beef mixture into loaves and top with mushroom slices.
3. Insert the drip tray into the bottom of the unit.
4. Spray the air rack with cooking spray and arrange the loaves on the air rack. Place air rack into unit by sliding through the side grooves and onto the back lip.
5. Press the On/Off button, select Bake setting, set the temperature to 200°C and the cooking time to 25 minutes. Press the On/Off button again to begin cooking.
6. When the cooking is complete, transfer the loaves to a plate and cut into desired size wedges and serve warm.

Crispy Sirloin Steak

| PREP TIME: 15 minutes
| COOK TIME: 10 minutes

2 (170 g) sirloin steaks, pounded
135 g plain flour
120 g panko breadcrumbs
2 eggs
1 tsp. garlic powder
1 tsp. onion powder
Salt and black pepper, to taste

1. Place the flour in a shallow bowl and whisk the eggs in a second dish.
2. Mix the panko breadcrumbs and spices in a third bowl.
3. Rub the steaks with flour, dip into the eggs and coat with breadcrumb mixture.
4. Insert the drip tray into the bottom of the unit.
5. Spray the steaks with cooking spray and arrange the steaks on the air rack. Place air rack into unit by sliding through the side grooves and onto the back lip.
6. Press the On/Off button, select Steak setting, set the temperature to 180°C and the cooking time to 10 minutes. Press the On/Off button again to begin cooking, flipping once in between.
7. When the cooking is complete, transfer the steaks to a plate and cut into desired size slices to serve.

CHAPTER 5
POULTRY PERFECTION

Simple Turkey Breast

SERVES 6

| PREP TIME: 20 minutes
| COOK TIME: 45 minutes

60 ml olive oil
1 (1.5-kg) turkey breast
Salt and black pepper, as required

1. Season the turkey breast with salt and black pepper and drizzle with olive oil.
2. Insert the drip tray into the bottom of the unit.
3. Slide the rotisserie rod through the center of the turkey breast and secure the turkey breast with the rotisserie forks. Secure the rotisserie spit in the unit.
4. Press the On/Off button, set the temperature to 200ºC and the cooking time to 45 minutes. Select rotate function and press the On/Off button again to begin cooking.
5. When the cooking is complete, transfer the turkey breast to a platter and cut into desired size slices to serve.

Ginger Chicken Thighs

SERVES 4

| PREP TIME: 10 minutes
| COOK TIME: 15 minutes

Vegetable oil spray
2 tbsps. vegetable oil
454 g boneless, skinless chicken thighs, cut crosswise into thirds
15 g julienned peeled fresh ginger
1 tbsp. honey
1 tbsp. ketchup

1 tbsp. soy sauce
1 tsp. garam masala
1 tsp. ground turmeric
¼ tsp. salt
½ tsp. cayenne pepper
15 g chopped fresh coriander, for garnish

1. In a small bowl, combine the ginger, vegetable oil, honey, soy sauce, ketchup, garam masala, turmeric, salt, and cayenne. Whisk until well combined.
2. Place the chicken in a resealable plastic bag and pour the marinade over. Seal the bag and massage to cover all of the chicken with the marinade. Marinate at room temperature for 30 minutes or in the refrigerator for up to 24 hours.
3. Insert the drip tray into the bottom of the unit.
4. Spray the air rack with vegetable oil spray and add the chicken and as much of the marinade and julienned ginger as possible. Place air rack into unit by sliding through the side grooves and onto the back lip.
5. Press the On/Off button, select Leg setting, set the temperature to 180ºC and the cooking time to 15 minutes. Press the On/Off button again to begin cooking. Use a meat thermometer to ensure the chicken has reached an internal temperature of 75ºC.
6. When the cooking is complete, transfer the chicken to a plate and serve garnished with coriander.

Spiced Chicken Breasts

SERVES 4

| PREP TIME: 20 minutes
| COOK TIME: 23 minutes

45 g butter, melted
4 (170 g) boneless, skinless chicken breasts
¼ tsp. smoked paprika
¼ tsp. garlic powder
¼ tsp. onion powder
Salt and black pepper, as required

1. Mix the butter and spices in a bowl and coat the chicken breasts with this mixture.
2. Insert the drip tray into the bottom of the unit.
3. Arrange the chicken breasts on the air rack. Place air rack into unit by sliding through the side grooves and onto the back lip.
4. Press the On/Off button, select Leg setting, set the temperature to 175°C and the cooking time to 23 minutes. Press the On/Off button again to begin cooking, flipping once in between.
5. When the cooking is complete, transfer the chicken breasts into a serving platter and serve hot.

Buttermilk Chicken Legs

SERVES 3

| PREP TIME: 15 minutes
| COOK TIME: 25 minutes

15 ml olive oil
225 g chicken legs
270 g plain flour
235 ml buttermilk
1 tsp. onion powder
1 tsp. garlic powder
1 tsp. ground cumin
1 tsp. paprika
Salt and ground black pepper, as required

1. Mix the chicken legs and buttermilk in a large bowl and refrigerate for about 2 hours.
2. Combine the flour and spices in another bowl and dredge the chicken legs into this mixture.
3. Then dip the chicken legs into the buttermilk and coat again with the flour mixture.
4. Insert the drip tray into the bottom of the unit.
5. Arrange the chicken legs on the air rack and drizzle with the oil. Place air rack into unit by sliding through the side grooves and onto the back lip.
6. Press the On/Off button, select Leg setting, set the temperature to 180°C and the cooking time to 25 minutes. Press the On/Off button again to begin cooking.
7. When the cooking is complete, transfer the chicken legs to a serving platter and serve hot.

Spiced Roasted Whole Chicken

SERVES 4

| **PREP TIME:** 15 minutes
| **COOK TIME:** 1 hour

45 ml olive oil
1 (2¼ kg) whole chicken, necks and giblets removed
2 tsps. paprika
2 tsps. dried thyme
1 tsp. cayenne pepper
1 tsp. ground white pepper
1 tsp. garlic powder
1 tsp. onion powder
Salt and ground black pepper, as required

1. Mix the thyme, spices and other seasoning in a bowl.
2. Coat the chicken generously with the oil and rub with spice mixture.
3. Insert the drip tray into the bottom of the unit.
4. Truss the chicken. Slide the rotisserie rod through the center of the chicken and secure the chicken with the rotisserie forks. Secure the rotisserie spit in the unit.
5. Press the On/Off button, set the temperature to 180°C and the cooking time to 1 hour. Select rotate function and press the On/Off button again to begin cooking.
6. When the cooking is complete, transfer the chicken to a platter and serve.

BBQ Chicken Wings

SERVES 4

| **PREP TIME:** 10 minutes
| **COOK TIME:** 30 minutes

cooking spray
120 ml BBQ sauce
900 g chicken wings, cut into drumettes and flats

1. Insert the drip tray into the bottom of the unit.
2. Spray the chicken wings with cooking spray and arrange on the air rack. Place air rack into unit by sliding through the side grooves and onto the back lip.
3. Press the On/Off button, select Leg setting, set the temperature to 200°C and the cooking time to 30 minutes. Press the On/Off button again to begin cooking, flipping once in between.
4. When the cooking is complete, transfer the chicken wings onto a serving platter and drizzle with the BBQ sauce to serve.

Chinese Chicken Drumsticks

SERVES 4

| PREP TIME: 15 minutes
| COOK TIME: 20 minutes

cooking spray
4 (170 g) chicken drumsticks
15 ml oyster sauce
1 tsp. light soy sauce
1 tsp. Chinese five spice powder
½ tsp. sesame oil
Salt and white pepper, as required

1. Mix the sauces, sesame oil, five spice powder, salt, and black pepper in a bowl.
2. Rub the chicken drumsticks with marinade and refrigerate for about 40 minutes.
3. Insert the drip tray into the bottom of the unit.
4. Spray the drumsticks with cooking spray and arrange on the air rack. Place air rack into unit by sliding through the side grooves and onto the back lip.
5. Press the On/Off button, select Leg setting, set the temperature to 200°C and the cooking time to 20 minutes. Press the On/Off button again to begin cooking, flipping once in between.
6. When the cooking is complete, transfer the chicken drumsticks onto a serving platter and serve hot.

Chicken and Pepper Kebabs

SERVES 4

| PREP TIME: 20 minutes
| COOK TIME: 12 minutes

cooking spray
4 (115 g) skinless, boneless chicken thighs, cubed into 2.5-cm size
2 bell peppers, cut into 2.5-cm pieces lengthwise
60 ml light soy sauce
15 ml mirin
1 tsp. sugar
1 tsp. garlic salt
Wooden skewers, pre-soaked

1. Mix the soy sauce, mirin, garlic salt, and sugar in a large baking dish.
2. Thread the chicken cubes and bell peppers onto pre-soaked wooden skewers.
3. Coat the skewers generously with this marinade and refrigerate for about 3 hours.
4. Insert the drip tray into the bottom of the unit.
5. Spray the skewers with cooking spray and arrange on the air rack. Place air rack into unit by sliding through the side grooves and onto the back lip.
6. Press the On/Off button, set the temperature to 180°C and the cooking time to 12 minutes. Press the On/Off button again to begin cooking.
7. When the cooking is complete, transfer the skewers to a platter and serve warm.

Cheese Spinach Stuffed Chicken Breasts

SERVES 2

| PREP TIME: 15 minutes
| COOK TIME: 29 minutes

cooking spray
15 ml olive oil
2 (115 g) skinless, boneless chicken breasts
65 g ricotta cheese, shredded
50 g fresh spinach
2 tbsps. cheddar cheese, grated
¼ tsp. paprika
Salt and ground black pepper, as required

1. Heat the olive oil in a medium frying pan over medium heat and cook the spinach for about 4 minutes.
2. Add the ricotta cheese and cook for about 1 minute.
3. Cut the slits in each chicken breast horizontally and stuff with the spinach mixture.
4. Season each chicken breast evenly with salt and black pepper and top with cheddar cheese and paprika.
5. Insert the drip tray into the bottom of the unit.
6. Spray the chicken breasts with cooking spray and arrange on the air rack. Place air rack into unit by sliding through the side grooves and onto the back lip.
7. Press the On/Off button, select Leg setting, set the temperature to 200ºC and the cooking time to 25 minutes. Press the On/Off button again to begin cooking.
8. When the cooking is complete, transfer the chicken breasts to a plate and serve hot.

Breaded Chicken Tenderloins

SERVES 4

| PREP TIME: 15 minutes
| COOK TIME: 12 minutes

cooking spray
30 ml rapeseed oil
8 skinless, boneless chicken tenderloins
1 egg, beaten
60 g panko breadcrumbs

1. Whisk the beaten egg in a bowl and mix the rapeseed oil and breadcrumbs in another bowl.
2. Dip the chicken tenderloins into the whisked egg and then coat with the breadcrumb mixture.
3. Insert the drip tray into the bottom of the unit.
4. Spray the chicken tenderloins with cooking spray and arrange on the air rack. Place air rack into unit by sliding through the side grooves and onto the back lip.
5. Press the On/Off button, set the temperature to 180ºC and the cooking time to 12 minutes. Press the On/Off button again to begin cooking, flipping once in between.
6. When the cooking is complete, transfer the chicken tenderloins into a platter and serve hot.

CHAPTER 6
HEALTHY SALADS

Apple Brussels Sprouts Salad

PREP TIME: 20 minutes
COOK TIME: 15 minutes

15 ml olive oil
450 g fresh medium Brussels sprouts, trimmed and halved vertically
2 apples, cored and chopped
220 g lettuce, torn
1 red onion, sliced
Salt and ground black pepper, as required
For the Dressing:
30 ml extra-virgin olive oil
30 ml fresh lemon juice
15 ml apple cider vinegar
20 g honey
1 tsp. Dijon mustard
Salt and ground black pepper, as required

1. Mix the Brussels sprouts, olive oil, salt, and black pepper in a large bowl and toss to coat well.
2. Insert the drip tray into the bottom of the unit.
3. Arrange the Brussels sprouts on the air rack. Place air rack into unit by sliding through the side grooves and onto the back lip.
4. Press the On/Off button, select Vegetable setting, set the temperature to 180°C and the cooking time to 15 minutes. Press the On/Off button again to begin cooking, flipping once in between.
5. When the cooking is complete, transfer the Brussels sprouts in a serving bowl and keep aside to cool.
6. Add the chopped apples, onion, and lettuce and combine well.
7. Mix all the dressing ingredients in a bowl and pour over the salad. Toss to coat well and enjoy.

Mixed Veggies Salad

PREP TIME: 25 minutes
COOK TIME: 40 minutes

60 ml olive oil, divided
3 medium carrots, cut into 1-cm thick rounds
3 small radishes, sliced into 1-cm thick rounds
2 red bell peppers, seeded and chopped
8 cherry tomatoes, cut in eighths
115 ml Italian dressing
60 g Parmesan cheese, grated
30 g green lentils, cooked
Salt, as required

1. Mix the carrots and 15 ml olive oil in a bowl and toss to coat well.
2. Mix the radishes and 15 ml olive oil in another bowl and toss to coat well.
3. Insert the drip tray into the bottom of the unit.
4. Arrange the carrots on one air rack and place the radishes on the other air rack. Place air racks into unit by sliding through the side grooves and onto the back lip.
5. Press the On/Off button, select Vegetable setting, set the temperature to 185°C and the cooking time to 40 minutes. Press the On/Off button again to begin cooking.
6. After 25 minutes, press the On/Off button, transfer the carrots to a bowl and set aside to cool. Place the cherry tomatoes on the rack. Set the temperature to 185°C and press the On/Off button to continue cooking.
7. When the cooking is complete, combine all the cooked vegetables.
8. Stir in the remaining ingredients except the Parmesan cheese and refrigerate covered for at least 2 hours. Garnish with Parmesan cheese and serve.

Potato and Celery Salad

| PREP TIME: 10 minutes
| COOK TIME: 40 minutes

cooking spray
15 ml olive oil
4 Rooster potatoes
3 hard-boiled eggs, peeled and chopped
225 g celery, chopped
60 ml mayonnaise
25 g red onion, chopped
15 ml prepared mustard
¼ tsp. celery salt
¼ tsp. garlic salt
Salt, as required

1. Prick the potatoes with a fork and rub with olive oil and salt.
2. Insert the drip tray into the bottom of the unit.
3. Spray the air rack with cooking spray and arrange the potatoes on the air rack. Place air rack into unit by sliding through the side grooves and onto the back lip.
4. Press the On/Off button, select Vegetable setting, set the temperature to 200°C and the cooking time to 40 minutes. Press the On/Off button again to begin cooking.
5. When the cooking is complete, transfer the potatoes in a serving bowl and keep aside to cool.
6. Add the remaining ingredients and combine well. Refrigerate for about 2 hours and serve immediately.

Feta Courgette Salad

| PREP TIME: 15 minutes
| COOK TIME: 30 minutes

cooking spray
60 ml olive oil
450 g courgette, cut into rounds
300 g fresh spinach, chopped
30 g feta cheese, crumbled
30 ml fresh lemon juice
1 tsp. garlic powder
Salt and black pepper, as required

1. Mix the courgette, olive oil, garlic powder, salt, and black pepper in a bowl and toss to coat well.
2. Insert the drip tray into the bottom of the unit.
3. Spray the air rack with cooking spray and arrange the courgette slices. Place air rack into unit by sliding through the side grooves and onto the back lip.
4. Press the On/Off button, select Vegetable setting, set the temperature to 200°C and the cooking time to 30 minutes. Press the On/Off button again to begin cooking, flipping thrice in between.
5. When the cooking is complete, transfer the courgette slices in a serving bowl and set aside to cool.
6. Add the spinach, feta cheese, lemon juice, a little bit of salt and black pepper in the serving bowl and combine well. Toss to coat well and serve immediately.

Aubergine Salad with Avocado

SERVES 2

| PREP TIME: 15 minutes
| COOK TIME: 15 minutes

1 aubergine, cut into 1-cm-thick slices crosswise
1 avocado, peeled, pitted and chopped
30 ml rapeseed oil
1 tsp. fresh lemon juice
Salt and ground black pepper, as required
For the Dressing:
15 ml extra-virgin olive oil
20 g honey
15 ml red wine vinegar
1 tbsp. fresh oregano leaves, chopped
1 tsp. Dijon mustard
1 tsp. fresh lemon zest, grated
Salt and ground black pepper, as required

1. Mix the aubergine, oil, salt, and black pepper in a large bowl and toss to coat well.
2. Insert the drip tray into the bottom of the unit.
3. Arrange the aubergines pieces on the air rack. Place air rack into unit by sliding through the side grooves and onto the back lip.
4. Press the On/Off button, select Vegetable setting, set the temperature to 200ºC and the cooking time to 15 minutes. Press the On/Off button again to begin cooking, flipping twice in between.
5. When the cooking is complete, transfer the aubergines in a serving bowl and keep aside to cool.
6. Add the avocado and lemon juice and mix well.
7. Mix all the dressing ingredients for in a bowl and pour over the salad. Toss to coat well and serve immediately.

Cauliflower Salad

SERVES 4

| PREP TIME: 20 minutes
| COOK TIME: 10 minutes

120 ml olive oil	**1 tbsp. curry powder**
1 head cauliflower, cut into small florets	**Salt, to taste**
235 ml boiling water	**For the Dressing:**
40 g spinach	**235 ml mayonnaise**
35 g pecans, toasted and chopped	**25 g sugar**
2 tbsps. fresh mint leaves, chopped	**15 ml fresh lemon juice**

1. Mix the cauliflower, pecans, curry powder, salt, and olive oil in a large bowl and toss to coat well.
2. Insert the drip tray into the bottom of the unit.
3. Arrange the cauliflower florets on the air rack. Place air rack into unit by sliding through the side grooves and onto the back lip.
4. Press the On/Off button, select Vegetable setting, set the temperature to 200ºC and the cooking time to 10 minutes. Press the On/Off button again to begin cooking, flipping once in between.
5. When the cooking is complete, transfer the cauliflower florets in a serving bowl and keep aside to cool.
6. Meanwhile, add the spinach in boiling water in a bowl for about 5 minutes.
7. Drain the sultanas well and combine with the cauliflower florets.
8. Mix all the dressing ingredients in a bowl and pour over the salad. Toss to coat well and serve immediately.

Fig, Chickpea and Rocket Salad

| PREP TIME: 15 minutes
| COOK TIME: 10 minutes

2 tbsps. extra-virgin olive oil, plus more for greasing
8 fresh figs, halved
260 g cooked chickpeas
60 g rocket, washed and dried
4 tbsps. balsamic vinegar
1 tsp. crushed roasted cumin seeds
Salt and ground black pepper, to taste

1. In a bowl, combine the chickpeas and cumin seeds.
2. Insert the drip tray into the bottom of the unit.
3. Grease the air racks lightly with oil. Arrange the figs on one air rack and the chickpeas on the other air racks. Place air racks into unit by sliding through the side grooves and onto the back lip.
4. Press the On/Off button, select Vegetable setting, set the temperature to 190°C and the cooking time to 10 minutes. Press the On/Off button again to begin cooking, shaking halfway through.
5. In the meantime, prepare the dressing. Mix the balsamic vinegar, olive oil, salt and pepper in a small bowl.
6. When the cooking is complete, remove the figs and chickpeas.
7. In a salad bowl, combine the rocket with the cooled figs and chickpeas. Toss with the dressing and serve.

Radish and Mozzarella Salad

| PREP TIME: 15 minutes
| COOK TIME: 30 minutes

cooking spray
30 ml olive oil
680 g radishes, trimmed and halved
230 g fresh mozzarella, sliced
1 tsp. honey
Salt and freshly ground black pepper, to taste

1. Mix the radishes, mozzarella, salt, black pepper and olive oil in a large bowl and toss to coat well.
2. Insert the drip tray into the bottom of the unit.
3. Spray the air rack with cooking spray and arrange the radish mixture. Place air rack into unit by sliding through the side grooves and onto the back lip.
4. Press the On/Off button, select Vegetable setting, set the temperature to 175°C and the cooking time to 30 minutes. Press the On/Off button again to begin cooking, flipping twice in between.
5. When the cooking is complete, transfer the radishes to a serving bowl and top with the remaining ingredients to serve.

Pork Neck Salad

PREP TIME: 20 minutes **COOK TIME:** 12 minutes	cooking spray 230 g pork neck 1 red onion, sliced 1 ripe tomato, thickly sliced 1 spring onion, chopped 15 ml fish sauce 15 ml soy sauce 7 ml oyster sauce 1 bunch fresh basil leaves

1. Mix all the sauces in a small bowl and coat the pork neck with the sauce mixture. Refrigerate for about 3 hours.
2. Insert the drip tray into the bottom of the unit.
3. Spray the air rack with cooking spray and arrange the pork neck on the air rack. Place air rack into unit by sliding through the side grooves and onto the back lip.
4. Press the On/Off button, select Ribs setting, set the temperature to 170ºC and the cooking time to 12 minutes. Press the On/Off button again to begin cooking, flipping once in between.
5. When the cooking is complete, transfer the pork neck in a platter. Cut into desired size slices and keep aside.
6. Mix the rest of the ingredients in a bowl and top with the pork slices and serve.

Lush Vegetable Salad

PREP TIME: 15 minutes **COOK TIME:** 15 minutes	cooking spray 1 tbsp. extra-virgin olive oil 6 plum tomatoes, halved 4 long red pepper, sliced 2 yellow pepper, sliced 2 large red onions, sliced 6 cloves garlic, crushed ½ lemon, juiced 1 tbsp. baby capers 1 tsp. paprika Salt and ground black pepper, to taste

1. Add the tomatoes, onions, peppers, and garlic in a large bowl and mix with the extra-virgin olive oil, paprika, and lemon juice. Sprinkle with salt and pepper to taste.
2. Insert the drip tray into the bottom of the unit.
3. Spray the air rack with cooking spray and arrange the vegetables on the air rack. Place air rack into unit by sliding through the side grooves and onto the back lip.
4. Press the On/Off button, select Vegetable setting, set the temperature to 200ºC and the cooking time to 15 minutes. Press the On/Off button again to begin cooking, shaking halfway through.
5. When the cooking is complete, transfer to a salad bowl and serve with the baby capers.

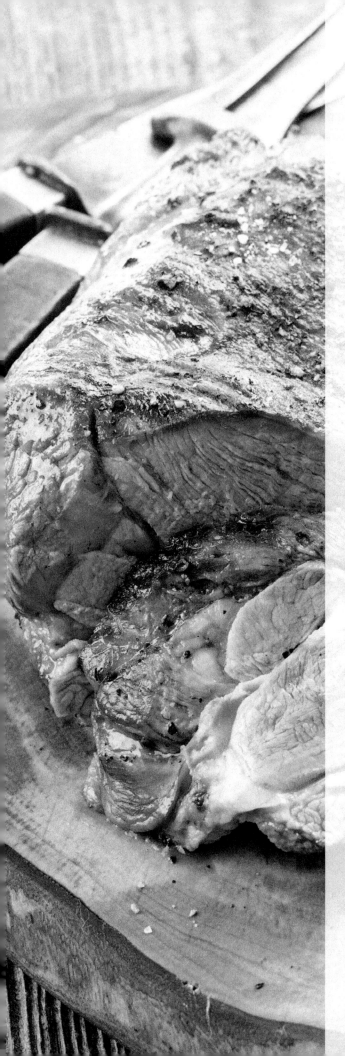

CHAPTER 7
LUSCIOUS LAMB

Nut Crusted Rack of Lamb

SERVES 6

| PREP TIME: 15 minutes
| COOK TIME: 30 minutes

cooking spray
15 ml olive oil
1 (340 g) rack of lamb
85 g almonds, chopped finely
1 egg
1 garlic clove, minced
1 tbsp. Panko breadcrumbs
1 tbsp. fresh rosemary, chopped
Salt and black pepper, to taste

1. Mix the garlic, olive oil, salt and black pepper in a bowl.
2. Whisk the egg in a shallow dish and combine the breadcrumbs, almonds and rosemary in another shallow dish.
3. Coat the rack of lamb with this garlic mixture evenly, dip into the egg and dredge into the breadcrumb mixture.
4. Insert the drip tray into the bottom of the unit.
5. Spray the rack of lamb with cooking spray and arrange on the air rack. Place air rack into unit by sliding through the side grooves and onto the back lip.
6. Press the On/Off button, select Ribs setting, set the temperature to 200ºC and the cooking time to 30 minutes. Press the On/Off button again to begin cooking.
7. When the cooking is complete, transfer the rack of lamb to a plate and serve warm.

Spiced Lamb Steaks

SERVES 3

| PREP TIME: 15 minutes
| COOK TIME: 15 minutes

cooking spray
680 g boneless lamb sirloin steaks
½ onion, roughly chopped
5 garlic cloves, peeled
1 tbsp. fresh ginger, peeled
1 tsp. garam masala
1 tsp. ground fennel
½ tsp. ground cinnamon
½ tsp. ground cumin
½ tsp. cayenne pepper
Salt and black pepper, to taste

1. Add the onion, garlic, ginger, and spices in a blender and pulse until smooth.
2. Coat the lamb steaks with this mixture on both sides and refrigerate to marinate for about 24 hours.
3. Insert the drip tray into the bottom of the unit.
4. Spray the lamb steaks with cooking spray and arrange on the air rack. Place air rack into unit by sliding through the side grooves and onto the back lip.
5. Press the On/Off button, select Steak setting, set the temperature to 165ºC and the cooking time to 15 minutes. Press the On/Off button again to begin cooking, flipping once in between.
6. When the cooking is complete, transfer the steaks in a platter and serve warm.

Spicy Lamb Kebabs

SERVES 6

| PREP TIME: 20 minutes
| COOK TIME: 8 minutes

30 ml olive oil
450 g lamb mince
4 eggs, beaten
150 g pistachios, chopped
35 g plain flour
4 garlic cloves, minced
30 ml fresh lemon juice
4 tbsps. flat-leaf parsley, chopped

2 tsps. chilli flakes
2 tsps. dried mint
2 tsps. salt
2 tsps. cumin seeds
1 tsp. fennel seeds
1 tsp. coriander seeds
1 tsp. freshly ground black pepper

1. Mix the lamb, eggs, pistachios, lemon juice, chilli flakes, flour, mint, parsley, cumin seeds, fennel seeds, coriander seeds, salt and black pepper in a large bowl.
2. Thread the lamb mixture onto metal skewers to form sausages and coat with olive oil.
3. Insert the drip tray into the bottom of the unit.
4. Arrange the skewers on the air rack. Place air rack into unit by sliding through the side grooves and onto the back lip.
5. Press the On/Off button, set the temperature to 180ºC and the cooking time to 8 minutes. Press the On/Off button again to begin cooking, flipping once in between.
6. When the cooking is complete, transfer the skewers to a platter and serve hot.

Roasted Lamb Leg

SERVES 4

| PREP TIME: 15 minutes
| COOK TIME: 1 hour

15 ml olive oil
1¼-kg half lamb leg roast, slits carved
2 garlic cloves, sliced into smaller slithers
1 tbsp. dried rosemary
Cracked Himalayan rock salt and cracked peppercorns, to taste

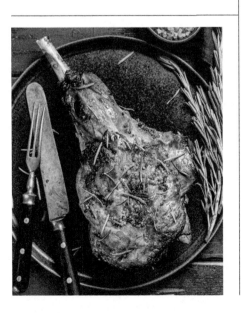

1. Insert the garlic slithers in the slits and brush with rosemary, olive oil, salt, and black pepper.
2. Insert the drip tray into the bottom of the unit.
3. Slide the rotisserie rod through the center of the lamb and secure the lamb with the rotisserie forks. Secure the rotisserie spit in the unit.
4. Press the On/Off button, set the temperature to 200ºC and the cooking time to 1 hour. Select rotate function and press the On/Off button again to begin cooking.
5. When the cooking is complete, transfer the lamb to a plate and serve hot.

Lamb Chops with Mint Pesto

SERVES 4

| PREP TIME: 15 minutes
| COOK TIME: 8 minutes

120 ml olive oil
50 g shelled pistachios
22 g grated Parmesan cheese
½ small clove garlic
1 tbsp. dried rosemary, chopped
1 tbsp. dried thyme
50 g packed fresh mint

15 g packed fresh parsley
½ tsp. lemon juice
¼ tsp. salt
8 lamb chops (1 rack)
2 tbsps. vegetable oil
Salt and freshly ground black pepper,
to taste

1. Make the pesto by combining the garlic, parsley and mint in a food processor and process until finely chopped. Add the lemon juice, Parmesan cheese, pistachios and ¼ tsp. salt. Process until all the ingredients have turned into a paste. With the processor running, gently pour the olive oil in. Scrape the sides of the processor with a spatula and process for another 30 seconds.
2. Rub the lamb chops with vegetable oil on both sides and season with salt, pepper, rosemary and thyme, pressing the herbs into the meat gently with the fingers.
3. Insert the drip tray into the bottom of the unit.
4. Arrange the lamb chops on the air rack. Place air rack into unit by sliding through the side grooves and onto the back lip.
5. Press the On/Off button, select Steak setting, set the temperature to 200ºC and the cooking time to 8 minutes. Press the On/Off button again to begin cooking, flipping once in between.
6. When the cooking is complete, transfer the lamb chops to a plate and drizzle with mint pesto. Serve warm.

Lamb with Potatoes

SERVES 2

| PREP TIME: 20 minutes
| COOK TIME: 25 minutes

cooking spray
5 ml olive oil
230 g lamb meat
2 small potatoes, peeled and halved
½ small onion, peeled and halved
15 g frozen sweet potato chips
1 garlic clove, crushed
½ tbsp. dried rosemary, crushed

1. Rub the lamb evenly with garlic and rosemary.
2. Insert the drip tray into the bottom of the unit.
3. Spray the lamb with cooking spray and arrange on the air rack. Place air rack into unit by sliding through the side grooves and onto the back lip.
4. Press the On/Off button, set the temperature to 180ºC and the cooking time to 10 minutes. Press the On/Off button again to begin cooking.
5. Meanwhile, microwave the potatoes for about 4 minutes. Transfer the potatoes in a large bowl and stir in the olive oil and onions.
6. When the cooking is complete, place the potato mixture on the other air rack and insert into the unit.
7. Press the On/Off button, set the temperature to 180ºC and the cooking time to 15 minutes. Press the On/Off button again to begin cooking, flipping once in between.
8. Once cooked, transfer the lamb and potato to a plate and serve hot.

Scrumptious Lamb Chops

SERVES 4

| PREP TIME: 20 minutes
| COOK TIME: 10 minutes

45 ml olive oil
4 (170 g) lamb chops
2 carrots, peeled and cubed
1 parsnip, peeled and cubed
1 fennel bulb, cubed
1 garlic clove, minced
2 tbsps. fresh mint leaves, minced
2 tbsps. dried rosemary
Salt and black pepper, to taste

1. Mix the herbs, garlic and olive oil in a large bowl and coat the lamb chops generously with this mixture.
2. Marinate in the refrigerator for about 3 hours.
3. Soak the vegetables in a large pan of water for about 15 minutes.
4. Insert the drip tray into the bottom of the unit.
5. Spray the air racks with cooking spray. Arrange the chop on one air rack and the vegetables on the other air rack. Place air racks into unit by sliding through the side grooves and onto the back lip.
6. Press the On/Off button, select Steak setting, set the temperature to 200ºC and the cooking time to 10 minutes. Press the On/Off button again to begin cooking.
7. With 2 minutes remaining, press the On/Off button, remove the vegetables and set aside to cool. Press the On/Off button again to continue cooking.
8. When the cooking is complete, transfer the chops to a plate and serve with vegetables.

Italian Lamb Chops with Avocado Mayo

SERVES 2

| PREP TIME: 5 minutes
| COOK TIME: 12 minutes

cooking spray
2 lamb chops
2 avocados
115 g mayonnaise
2 tsps. Italian herbs
1 tbsp. lemon juice

1. Season the lamb chops with the Italian herbs, then set aside for about 5 minutes.
2. Insert the drip tray into the bottom of the unit.
3. Spray the chops with cooking spray and arrange on the air rack. Place air rack into unit by sliding through the side grooves and onto the back lip.
4. Press the On/Off button, select Steak setting, set the temperature to 200ºC and the cooking time to 12 minutes. Press the On/Off button again to begin cooking, flipping halfway through cooking.
5. In the meantime, halve the avocados and remove the pits. Spoon the flesh into a blender.
6. Add the mayonnaise and lemon juice and pulse until a smooth consistency is achieved.
7. When the cooking is complete, transfer the chops to a plate and serve with the avocado mayo.

Air Fried Lamb Ribs

SERVES 4

| PREP TIME: 5 minutes
| COOK TIME: 18 minutes

cooking spray
454 g lamb ribs
280 g Greek yoghurt
2 tbsps. mustard
15 g mint leaves, chopped
1 tsp. rosemary, chopped
Salt and ground black pepper, to taste

1. Use a brush to apply the mustard to the lamb ribs, and season with rosemary, salt, and black pepper.
2. Insert the drip tray into the bottom of the unit.
3. Spray the ribs with cooking spray and arrange on the air rack. Place air rack into unit by sliding through the side grooves and onto the back lip.
4. Press the On/Off button, select Ribs setting, set the temperature to 180ºC and the cooking time to 18 minutes. Press the On/Off button again to begin cooking, flipping once in between.
5. Meanwhile, combine the mint and Greek yoghurt in a bowl.
6. When the cooking is complete, transfer the lamb ribs to a plate and serve with the mint yoghurt.

Herbed Lamb Chops

SERVES 2

| PREP TIME: 10 minutes
| COOK TIME: 15 minutes

15 ml olive oil
4 (115 g) lamb chops
15 ml fresh lemon juice
1 tsp. dried oregano
1 tsp. dried rosemary
1 tsp. dried thyme
½ tsp. ground coriander
½ tsp. ground cumin
Salt and black pepper, to taste

1. Mix the lemon juice, olive oil, herbs, and spices in a large bowl.
2. Coat the lamb chops generously with the herb mixture and refrigerate to marinate for about 1 hour.
3. Insert the drip tray into the bottom of the unit.
4. Spray the chops with cooking spray and arrange on the air rack. Place air rack into unit by sliding through the side grooves and onto the back lip.
5. Press the On/Off button, select Steak setting, set the temperature to 200ºC and the cooking time to 15 minutes. Press the On/Off button again to begin cooking, flipping once in between.
6. When the cooking is complete, transfer the lamb chops in a platter and serve hot.

CHAPTER 8

PORK PALATE PLEASER

Pork Spare Ribs

| PREP TIME: 15 minutes
| COOK TIME: 20 minutes

60 ml olive oil
12 (2½-cm) pork spare ribs
115 ml rice vinegar
30 ml soy sauce
60 g cornflour
5-6 garlic cloves, minced
Salt and black pepper, to taste

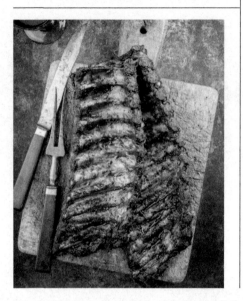

1. Mix the garlic, vinegar, soy sauce, salt and pepper in a large bowl.
2. Coat the ribs generously with this mixture and refrigerate to marinate overnight.
3. Place the cornflour in a shallow bowl and dredge the ribs in it.
4. Insert the drip tray into the bottom of the unit.
5. Drizzle the ribs with olive oil and arrange on the air rack. Place air rack into unit by sliding through the side grooves and onto the back lip.
6. Press the On/Off button, select Ribs setting, set the temperature to 200ºC and the cooking time to 20 minutes. Press the On/Off button again to begin cooking, flipping once in between.
7. When the cooking is complete, transfer the ribs to a plate and serve hot.

Garlic Butter Pork Chops

| PREP TIME: 10 minutes
| COOK TIME: 8 minutes

cooking spray
15 g coconut butter
4 pork chops
1 tbsp. coconut oil
2 tsps. parsley
2 tsps. garlic, grated
Salt and black pepper, to taste

1. Mix all the seasonings, coconut oil, butter, garlic, and parsley in a bowl and coat the pork chops evenly.
2. Cover the chops with aluminium foil and refrigerate to marinate for about 1 hour.
3. Insert the drip tray into the bottom of the unit.
4. Remove the foil and spray the chops with cooking spray. Arrange the chops on the air rack and place air rack into unit by sliding through the side grooves and onto the back lip.
5. Press the On/Off button, select Steak setting, set the temperature to 175ºC and the cooking time to 8 minutes. Press the On/Off button again to begin cooking, flipping once in between.
6. When the cooking is complete, transfer the chops to a plate and serve warm.

Aromatic Pork Loin Roast

SERVES 6

| **PREP TIME:** 55 minutes
| **COOK TIME:** 55 minutes

680 g boneless pork loin roast, washed
2 tbsps. lime juice
2 dried sprigs thyme, crushed
1 tsp. mustard seeds
1 tsp. garlic powder
1 tsp. porcini powder
1 tsp. shallot powder
1 tsp. red pepper flakes, crushed
¾ tsp. sea salt flakes

1. Firstly, score the meat with a small knife, make sure to not cut too deep.
2. In a small-sized mixing dish, combine all seasonings in the order listed above, mix to combine well.
3. Massage the spice mix into the pork meat to evenly distribute. Drizzle with lemon juice. Spray the pork with cooking spray
4. Insert the drip tray into the bottom of the unit.
5. Slide the rotisserie rod through the center of the pork and secure the pork with the rotisserie forks. Secure the rotisserie spit in the unit.
6. Press the On/Off button, set the temperature to 180°C and the cooking time to 50 minutes. Select rotate function and press the On/Off button again to begin cooking.
7. When the cooking is complete, transfer the pork to a plate and serve warm.

Spicy Pork Kebabs

SERVES 3

| **PREP TIME:** 22 minutes
| **COOK TIME:** 18 minutes

cooking spray
455 g pork mince
50 g spring onions, finely chopped
2 tbsps. tomato purée
3 cloves garlic, peeled and finely minced
1 tsp. ground black pepper, or more to taste
½ fresh serrano, minced
⅓ tsp. Paprika
1 lime, chopped
1 tsp. salt, or more to taste

1. Add all the ingredients in a mixing dish and combine well. Shape this mixture into sausages.
2. Insert the drip tray into the bottom of the unit.
3. Spray the sausages with cooking spray and arrange on the air rack. Place air rack into unit by sliding through the side grooves and onto the back lip.
4. Press the On/Off button, set the temperature to 180°C and the cooking time to 18 minutes. Press the On/Off button again to begin cooking, flipping once in between.
5. When the cooking is complete, mound lime on a serving platter, top with cooked kebabs and serve warm. Bon appétit!

Chinese Style Pork Meatballs

SERVES 3

| **PREP TIME:** 15 minutes
| **COOK TIME:** 10 minutes

cooking spray
170 g pork mince
1 egg, beaten
30 g cornflour
1 tsp. oyster sauce
½ tbsp. olive oil
½ tbsp. light soy sauce
½ tsp. sesame oil
¼ tsp. five spice powder
¼ tsp. brown sugar

1. Mix all the ingredients in a bowl except cornflour until well combined.
2. Shape the pork mixture into equal-sized balls and place the cornflour in a shallow dish.
3. Roll the meatballs evenly into cornflour mixture and spray with cooking spray.
4. Insert the drip tray into the bottom of the unit.
5. Arrange the meatballs on the air rack. Place air rack into unit by sliding through the side grooves and onto the back lip.
6. Press the On/Off button, set the temperature to 200ºC and the cooking time to 10 minutes. Press the On/Off button again to begin cooking.
7. When the cooking is complete, transfer the meatballs to a plate and serve warm.

Breaded Pork Chops

SERVES 2

| **PREP TIME:** 15 minutes
| **COOK TIME:** 15 minutes

cooking spray
15 ml rapeseed oil
2 (170 g) pork chops
115 g Panko breadcrumbs
35 g plain flour
1 egg
Salt and black pepper, to taste

1. Season the pork chops with salt and black pepper to taste.
2. Place the flour in a shallow bowl and whisk an egg in a second bowl.
3. Mix the breadcrumbs and rapeseed oil in a third bowl.
4. Coat the pork chops with flour, dip into egg and dredge into the breadcrumb mixture.
5. Insert the drip tray into the bottom of the unit.
6. Spray the chops with cooking spray and arrange on the air rack. Place air rack into unit by sliding through the side grooves and onto the back lip.
7. Press the On/Off button, select Steak setting, set the temperature to 200ºC and the cooking time to 15 minutes. Press the On/Off button again to begin cooking, flipping once in between.
8. When the cooking is complete, transfer the chops to a plate and serve hot.

Pork Casserole with Ricotta

SERVES 4

| PREP TIME: 25 minutes
| COOK TIME: 22 minutes

2 tbsps. olive oil
910 g pork tenderloin, cut into serving-size pieces
250 g Ricotta cheese
360 ml chicken stock
1 tbsp. mustard
1 tsp. dried marjoram
1 tsp. coarse sea salt
½ tsp. freshly ground pepper
¼ tsp. chilli powder

1. Heat the olive oil in a pan over medium-high heat. Once hot, cook the pork for 6 to 7 minutes, flipping it to ensure even cooking.
2. Arrange the pork in a lightly greased casserole dish. Season with salt, black pepper, chilli powder, and marjoram.
3. In a mixing dish, thoroughly combine the mustard, cheese, and chicken stock. Pour the mixture over the pork in the casserole dish.
4. Insert the drip tray into the bottom of the unit.
5. Arrange the casserole dish on the air rack. Place air rack into unit by sliding through the side grooves and onto the back lip.
6. Press the On/Off button, select Bake setting, set the temperature to 180ºC and the cooking time to 15 minutes. Press the On/Off button again to begin cooking, until bubbly and heated through.
7. When the cooking is complete, let the casserole dish cool for 5 minutes and serve warm.

Sun-dried Tomato Stuffed Pork Roll

SERVES 4

| PREP TIME: 20 minutes
| COOK TIME: 15 minutes

7 ml olive oil
4 (170 g) pork cutlets, pounded slightly
15 g sun-dried tomatoes, chopped finely
2 tbsps. fresh parsley, chopped
1 spring onion, chopped
2 tsps. paprika
Salt and freshly ground black pepper, to taste

1. Mix the spring onion, tomatoes, parsley, salt and black pepper in a bowl.
2. Coat each cutlet with this tomato mixture and roll up the cutlet, securing with cocktail sticks.
3. Coat the rolls with olive oil and rub with paprika, salt and black pepper.
4. Insert the drip tray into the bottom of the unit.
5. Arrange the rolls on the air rack. Place air rack into unit by sliding through the side grooves and onto the back lip.
6. Press the On/Off button, set the temperature to 200ºC and the cooking time to 15 minutes. Press the On/Off button again to begin cooking.
7. When the cooking is complete, transfer the rolls to a plate and serve warm.

Streaky Rasher Wrapped Pork Tenderloin

| PREP TIME: 15 minutes
| COOK TIME: 30 minutes

cooking spray
2 tbsps. Dijon mustard
4 streaky rashers
1 (680 g) pork tenderloin

1. Rub the pork tenderloin evenly with mustard and wrap the tenderloin with streaky rasher strips. Spray with cooking spray.
2. Insert the drip tray into the bottom of the unit.
3. Slide the rotisserie rod through the center of the pork tenderloin and secure the pork tenderloin with the rotisserie forks. Secure the rotisserie spit in the unit.
4. Press the On/Off button, set the temperature to 180ºC and the cooking time to 30 minutes. Select rotate function and press the On/Off button again to begin cooking.
5. When the cooking is complete, transfer the pork tenderloin to a plate and cut into desired size slices. Serve warm.

BBQ Pork Steaks

| PREP TIME: 5 minutes
| COOK TIME: 15 minutes

4 pork steaks
120 ml ketchup
110 g brown sugar
2 tbsps. BBQ sauce
1 tbsp. Cajun seasoning
1 tbsp. vinegar
1 tsp. soy sauce

1. Sprinkle the pork steaks with Cajun seasoning.
2. Combine the remaining ingredients in a bowl and brush onto the pork steaks.
3. Insert the drip tray into the bottom of the unit.
4. Spray the air rack with cooking spray and arrange the pork steaks on the air rack. Place air rack into unit by sliding through the side grooves and onto the back lip.
5. Press the On/Off button, select Steak setting, set the temperature to 180ºC and the cooking time to 15 minutes. Press the On/Off button again to begin cooking, flipping once in between.
6. When the cooking is complete, transfer the pork steaks to a plate and serve warm.

CHAPTER 9
STARTERS AND SNACKS

Avocado Chips

SERVES 2

| **PREP TIME:** 20 minutes
| **COOK TIME:** 7 minutes

cooking spray
1 avocado, peeled, pitted and sliced into 8 pieces
60 g panko breadcrumbs
1 egg
35 g plain flour
5 ml water
Salt and black pepper, to taste

1. Place the flour, salt and black pepper in a shallow dish and whisk the egg with water in a second dish. Put the breadcrumbs in a third shallow dish.
2. Coat the avocado slices evenly in flour and dip in the egg mixture. Roll into the breadcrumbs evenly.
3. Spray the avocado slices with cooking spray and place on the rotating mesh basket.
4. Insert the drip tray into the bottom of the unit.
5. Secure the rotating mesh basket on the unit. Press the On/Off button, select Fries setting, set the temperature to 200ºC and the cooking time to 7 minutes. Select rotate function and press the On/Off button again to begin cooking.
6. When the cooking is complete, transfer the avocado to a plate and serve warm.

Cheese Crisps

SERVES 2

| **PREP TIME:** 10 minutes
| **COOK TIME:** 12 minutes

1 egg white
50 g shredded Parmesan cheese

1. Place a piece of parchment paper in the bottom of the air rack.
2. In a medium bowl, combine the cheese and egg white, stirring with a fork until thoroughly combined.
3. Place small scoops of the cheese mixture in a single layer in the air rack, about 2-cm apart. Use the fork to spread the mixture as thin as possible.
4. Insert the drip tray into the bottom of the unit.
5. Arrange air rack into unit by sliding through the side grooves and onto the back lip.
6. Press the On/Off button, select Fries setting, set the temperature to 200ºC and the cooking time to 12 minutes. Press the On/Off button again to begin cooking, until the crisps are golden brown.
7. When the cooking is complete, let cool for a few minutes before transferring them to a plate. Enjoy!

Spiced Apple Crisps

SERVES 2

| PREP TIME: 10 minutes
| COOK TIME: 8 minutes

cooking spray
1 apple, peeled, cored and thinly sliced
15 g sugar
½ tsp. ground cinnamon
Pinch of ground ginger
Pinch of ground cardamom
Pinch of salt

1. Mix together all the ingredients in a medium bowl until well combined.
2. Spray the apple slices with cooking spray and place on the rotating mesh basket.
3. Insert the drip tray into the bottom of the unit.
4. Secure the rotating mesh basket on the unit. Press the On/Off button, select Fries setting, set the temperature to 200°C and the cooking time to 8 minutes. Select rotate function and press the On/Off button again to begin cooking.
5. When the cooking is complete, transfer the apple slices to a plate and enjoy.

Crispy Kale Crisps

SERVES 4

| PREP TIME: 10 minutes
| COOK TIME: 3 minutes

15 ml olive oil
1 head fresh kale, stems and ribs removed and cut into 4-cm pieces
1 tsp. soy sauce

1. Mix together all the ingredients in a bowl until well combined.
2. Place kale pieces on the rotating mesh basket.
3. Insert the drip tray into the bottom of the unit.
4. Secure the rotating mesh basket on the unit. Press the On/Off button, select Fries setting, set the temperature to 200°C and the cooking time to 3 minutes. Select rotate function and press the On/Off button again to begin cooking.
5. When the cooking is complete, transfer the kale to a serving bowl and serve warm.

Tortilla Crisps

| PREP TIME: 10 minutes
| COOK TIME: 5 minutes

cooking spray
15 ml olive oil
8 corn tortillas, cut into triangles
Salt, to taste

1. Drizzle the tortilla crisps with olive oil and season with salt to taste.
2. Spray the tortilla crisps with cooking spray and place on the rotating mesh basket.
3. Insert the drip tray into the bottom of the unit.
4. Secure the rotating mesh basket on the unit. Press the On/Off button, select Fries setting, set the temperature to 200ºC and the cooking time to 5 minutes. Select rotate function and press the On/Off button again to begin cooking.
5. When the cooking is complete, transfer the tortilla crisp and serve warm.

Courgette Fries

| PREP TIME: 10 minutes
| COOK TIME: 10 minutes

cooking spray
2 medium courgettes, ends removed, quartered lengthwise, and sliced into 6-cm long fries
75 g grated Parmesan cheese
70 g heavy whipping cream
50 g blanched finely ground almond flour
1 tsp. Italian seasoning
½ tsp. salt

1. Sprinkle the courgettes with salt and wrap in a kitchen towel to draw out excess moisture. Let it sit for about 2 hours.
2. Pour the cream into a medium bowl. In a separate medium bowl, whisk together flour, Parmesan cheese, and Italian seasoning.
3. Place each courgette fry into cream, then gently shake off excess. Press each fry into dry mixture, coating each side.
4. Spray the courgette fries with cooking spray and place on the rotating mesh basket.
5. Insert the drip tray into the bottom of the unit.
6. Secure the rotating mesh basket on the unit. Press the On/Off button, select Fries setting, set the temperature to 200ºC and the cooking time to 10 minutes. Select rotate function and press the On/Off button again to begin cooking. Fries will be golden and crispy when done.
7. When the cooking is complete, transfer the courgette fries on clean parchment sheet to cool for 5 minutes before serving.

Crispy Prawns

SERVES 2

| PREP TIME: 15 minutes
| COOK TIME: 8 minutes

cooking spray
10 prawns, peeled and deveined
1 egg
115 g nacho crisps, crushed
Salt and black pepper, to taste

1. Crack the egg in a shallow dish and beat well. Place the nacho crisps in another shallow dish.
2. Season the prawns with salt and black pepper, coat into egg and then roll into nacho crisps.
3. Spray the prawns with cooking spray and place on the rotating mesh basket.
4. Insert the drip tray into the bottom of the unit.
5. Secure the rotating mesh basket on the unit. Press the On/Off button, select Prawn setting, set the temperature to 180ºC and the cooking time to 8 minutes. Select rotate function and press the On/Off button again to begin cooking.
6. When the cooking is complete, transfer the prawns to a serving bowl and serve warm.

Chicken Nuggets

SERVES 4

| PREP TIME: 15 minutes
| COOK TIME: 10 minutes

cooking spray
560 g chicken breast, cut into chunks
135 g plain flour
120 g panko breadcrumbs
1 egg
30 ml milk
½ tbsp. mustard powder
1 tbsp. onion powder
1 tbsp. garlic powder
Salt and black pepper, to taste

1. Put the chicken chunks along with mustard powder, garlic powder, onion powder, salt and black pepper in a food processor and pulse until combined.
2. Add the flour in a shallow dish and whisk the eggs with milk in a second dish.
3. Place the breadcrumbs in a third shallow dish.
4. Shape the chicken mixture into nuggets. Coat the chicken nuggets evenly in flour and dip in the egg mixture. Then roll into the breadcrumbs evenly.
5. Insert the drip tray into the bottom of the unit.
6. Spray the air rack with cooking spray and arrange the nuggets on the air rack. Place air rack into unit by sliding through the side grooves and onto the back lip.
7. Press the On/Off button, set the temperature to 200ºC and the cooking time to 10 minutes. Press the On/Off button again to begin cooking, flipping once halfway through.
8. When the cooking is complete, transfer the nuggets to a bowl and serve warm.

Bacon Wrapped Onion Rings

SERVES 8

| PREP TIME: 5 minutes
| COOK TIME: 10 minutes

cooking spray
8 slices bacon
1 large white onion, peeled and cut into 16 (1/2-cm-thick) slices

1. Stack 2 slices onion and wrap with 1 slice bacon. Secure with a toothpick. Repeat with remaining onion slices and bacon.
2. Spray the onion rings with cooking spray and place on the rotating mesh basket.
3. Insert the drip tray into the bottom of the unit.
4. Secure the rotating mesh basket on the unit. Press the On/Off button, select Fries setting, set the temperature to 175°C and the cooking time to 10 minutes. Select rotate function and press the On/Off button again to begin cooking. Bacon will be crispy when done.
5. When the cooking is complete, transfer the onion rings to a plate and serve hot.

Ranch Pickle Spears

SERVES 4

| PREP TIME: 40 minutes
| COOK TIME: 10 minutes

cooking spray
4 dill pickle spears, halved lengthwise
60 ml ranch dressing
50 g grated Parmesan cheese
50 g blanched finely ground almond flour
2 tbsps. dry ranch seasoning

1. Wrap the pickle spears in a kitchen towel 30 minutes to soak up excess pickle juice.
2. Pour the ranch dressing into a medium bowl and add the pickle spears.
3. In a separate medium bowl, mix the flour, Parmesan, and ranch seasoning.
4. Remove each spear from ranch dressing and shake off excess. Press gently into dry mixture to coat all sides.
5. Spray the pickle spears with cooking spray and place on the rotating mesh basket.
6. Insert the drip tray into the bottom of the unit.
7. Secure the rotating mesh basket on the unit. Press the On/Off button, select Fries setting, set the temperature to 200°C and the cooking time to 10 minutes. Select rotate function and press the On/Off button again to begin cooking.
8. When the cooking is complete, transfer the pickle spears to a plate and serve warm.

CHAPTER 10
BAKING AND DESSERTS

Apple Doughnuts

| PREP TIME: 45 minutes
| COOK TIME: 20 minutes

cooking spray
30 g unsalted butter, softened
365 g plain flour
½ pink lady apple, peeled, cored and grated
235 ml sweet cider or apple juice

100 g brown sugar
1 egg
1½ tsps. baking powder
½ tsp. ground cinnamon
½ tsp. salt

1. Boil the apple cider in a medium pan over medium-high heat and reduce the heat.
2. Let it simmer for about 15 minutes and dish out in a bowl.
3. Sift together flour, baking powder, bread soda, cinnamon, and salt in a large bowl.
4. Combine the brown sugar, egg, cooled apple cider and butter in another bowl.
5. Stir in the flour mixture and grated apple and mix to form a dough.
6. Wrap the dough with a clingfilm and refrigerate for about 30 minutes.
7. Roll the dough into 2.5-cm thickness and cut the doughnuts with a doughnut cutter.
8. Insert the drip tray into the bottom of the unit.
9. Spray the air rack with cooking spray and arrange the doughnuts on the air rack. Place air rack into unit by sliding through the side grooves and onto the back lip.
10. Press the On/Off button, select Bake setting, set the temperature to 180°C and the cooking time to 5 minutes. Press the On/Off button again to begin cooking, flipping once in between.
11. When the cooking is complete, transfer the doughnuts to a plate and serve warm.

Homemade Blueberry Cake

| PREP TIME: 10 minutes
| COOK TIME: 25 minutes

cooking spray
3 eggs
135 g sugar
115 ml sour cream
115 g butter, room temperature
100 g almond flour
55 g blueberries
2 tsps. vanilla
1½ tsps. baking powder

1. Grease a cake pan lightly with cooking spray.
2. Mix all the ingredients in a bowl except the blueberries.
3. Pour the batter in the cake pan and fold in the blueberries. Mix well.
4. Insert the drip tray into the bottom of the unit.
5. Arrange the cake pan on the air rack. Place air rack into unit by sliding through the side grooves and onto the back lip.
6. Press the On/Off button, select Bake setting, set the temperature to 190°C and the cooking time to 25 minutes. Press the On/Off button again to begin cooking.
7. When the cooking is complete, transfer the cake to a plate and cut into slices to serve.

Tasty Cherry Pie

SERVES 4

| PREP TIME: 20 minutes
| COOK TIME: 20 minutes

300 g tinned cherry fruit filling
1 refrigerated pre-made shortcrust pastry shell
7 ml milk
1 egg yolk
15 ml rapeseed oil

1. Grease a pie crust with rapeseed oil.
2. Press the pie crust into a pie dish and poke the holes with a fork all over dough.
3. Insert the drip tray into the bottom of the unit.
4. Arrange the pie dish on the air rack. Place air rack into unit by sliding through the side grooves and onto the back lip.
5. Press the On/Off button, select Bake setting, set the temperature to 160ºC and the cooking time to 20 minutes. Press the On/Off button again to begin cooking.
6. After 5 minutes, press the On/Off button, pour the cherry fruit filling into pie crust. Cut the remaining pie crust into 2-cm strips and place the strips in a crisscross manner. Whisk the egg and milk in a small bowl and brush the egg wash on the top of pie. Press the On/Off button again to continue cooking.
7. When the cooking is complete, transfer the pie dish and serve warm.

Chocolate Mug Cake

SERVES 1

| PREP TIME: 15 minutes
| COOK TIME: 13 minutes

cooking spray
45 g coconut oil
75 g caster sugar
45 ml milk
35 g self raising flour
10 g cocoa powder

1. Grease a large mug lightly with cooking spray.
2. Mix all the ingredients in a shallow mug until well combined.
3. Insert the drip tray into the bottom of the unit.
4. Arrange the mug on the air rack. Place air rack into unit by sliding through the side grooves and onto the back lip.
5. Press the On/Off button, select Bake setting, set the temperature to 200ºC and the cooking time to 13 minutes. Press the On/Off button again to begin cooking.
6. When the cooking is complete, let the mug cake cool for 5 minutes and serve warm.

Dark Chocolate Cake

SERVES 4

| PREP TIME: 10 minutes
| COOK TIME: 10 minutes

cooking spray
2 eggs
100 g unsalted butter
100 g sugar free dark chocolate, chopped
50 g sugar
10 g almond flour

1. Grease 4 regular sized ramekins with cooking spray.
2. Microwave all chocolate bits with butter in a bowl for about 3 minutes.
3. Remove from the microwave and whisk in the eggs and sugar.
4. Stir in the flour and combine well until smooth.
5. Insert the drip tray into the bottom of the unit.
6. Transfer the mixture into the ramekins and arrange on the air rack. Place air rack into unit by sliding through the side grooves and onto the back lip.
7. Press the On/Off button, select Bake setting, set the temperature to 190ºC and the cooking time to 10 minutes. Press the On/Off button again to begin cooking.
8. When the cooking is complete, transfer the ramekins and serve warm.

Raspberry Cupcakes

SERVES 10

| PREP TIME: 15 minutes
| COOK TIME: 15 minutes

cooking spray
2 eggs
135 g butter, softened
125 g self raising flour
125 g caster sugar
80 g fresh raspberries
15 g cream cheese, softened
10 ml fresh lemon juice
½ tsp. baking powder
A pinch of salt

1. Grease 10 silicon cups lightly with cooking spray.
2. Mix the flour, baking powder, and salt in a large bowl until well combined.
3. Stir well the cream cheese, sugar, eggs, raspberries, butter, lemon juice and flour mixture in another bowl.
4. Insert the drip tray into the bottom of the unit.
5. Transfer the mixture into silicon cups and arrange on the air rack. Place air rack into unit by sliding through the side grooves and onto the back lip.
6. Press the On/Off button, select Cupcake setting, set the temperature to 160ºC and the cooking time to 15 minutes. Press the On/Off button again to begin cooking.
7. When the cooking is complete, invert the cupcakes onto wire rack to completely cool.

Sunflower Seeds Bread

SERVES 4

| PREP TIME: 15 minutes
| COOK TIME: 18 minutes

cooking spray
235 ml lukewarm water
90 g plain flour
90 g fine wholemeal flour
45 g sunflower seeds
½ sachet instant yeast
1 tsp. salt

1. Grease a cake pan with cooking spray.
2. Mix together flours, sunflower seeds, yeast and salt in a large bowl.
3. Add the water slowly and knead for about 5 minutes until a dough is formed.
4. Cover the dough with a clingfilm and keep in warm place for about 30 minutes.
5. Insert the drip tray into the bottom of the unit.
6. Arrange the cake pan on the air rack. Place air rack into unit by sliding through the side grooves and onto the back lip.
7. Press the On/Off button, select Bake setting, set the temperature to 200°C and the cooking time to 18 minutes. Press the On/Off button again to begin cooking.
8. When the cooking is complete, let the bread cool for 10 minutes and serve.

Sweet Potato Pie

SERVES 4

| PREP TIME: 15 minutes
| COOK TIME: 1 hour

cooking spray
5 ml olive oil
1 prepared shortcrust pastry, thawed
170 g sweet potato
2 large eggs
60 ml double cream
30 ml maple syrup
15 g butter, melted
1 tbsp. brown sugar
¾ tsp. vanilla extract
½ tsp. ground cinnamon
1/8 tsp. ground nutmeg
Salt, to taste

1. Grease a pie dish with cooking spray.
2. Rub the sweet potato with olive oil.
3. Insert the drip tray into the bottom of the unit.
4. Arrange the sweet potato on the air rack. Place air rack into unit by sliding through the side grooves and onto the back lip.
5. Press the On/Off button, select Vegetable setting, set the temperature to 200°C and the cooking time to 30 minutes. Press the On/Off button again to begin cooking.
6. When the cooking is complete, transfer the sweet potato to a bowl.
7. Let cool and mash it completely.
8. Add the rest of the ingredients and mix until well combined.
9. Arrange the shell into the greased pie dish and place the mixture over the pie shell.
10. Transfer the pie dish on the air rack. Place air rack into unit by sliding through the side grooves and onto the back lip.
11. Press the On/Off button, select Bake setting, set the temperature to 200°C and the cooking time to 30 minutes. Press the On/Off button again to begin cooking.
12. When the cooking is complete, let cool for 10 minutes and serve warm.

Vanilla Soufflé

PREP TIME: 15 minutes COOK TIME: 27 minutes	235 ml milk 4 egg yolks 5 egg whites 125 g sugar, divided 60 g butter, softened 35 g plain flour 3 tsps. vanilla extract, divided 1 tsp. cream of tartar

1. Grease 6 ramekins lightly with cooking spray.
2. Mix the butter and flour in a bowl until a smooth paste is formed.
3. Put the milk and 100 g sugar in a pot on medium-low heat and cook for about 3 minutes.
4. Bring to a boil and stir in the flour mixture.
5. Let it simmer for 4 minutes and turn off the heat.
6. Whisk the egg yolks and vanilla extract in a bowl until well combined.
7. Combine the egg yolk mixture with milk mixture until well mixed.
8. Mix the egg whites, cream of tartar, remaining sugar and vanilla extract in another bowl.
9. Combine the egg white mixture into milk mixture and divide this mixture evenly into the ramekins.
10. Insert the drip tray into the bottom of the unit.
11. Arrange the 3 ramekins on each air rack. Place the air racks into unit by sliding through the side grooves and onto the back lip.
12. Press the On/Off button, select Bake setting, set the temperature to 165ºC and the cooking time to 20 minutes. Press the On/Off button again to begin cooking.
13. When the cooking is complete, transfer the ramekins and serve warm.

Homemade Chocolate Croissants

PREP TIME: 10 minutes COOK TIME: 12 minutes	Cooking spray 100 g chocolate-hazelnut spread 1 large egg, beaten 1 sheet frozen puff pastry, thawed

1. Roll the puff pastry into a 28-cm square on a lightly floured surface. Cut pastry into quarters to form 4 squares. Cut each square diagonally to form 8 triangles.
2. Spread 2 tsps. chocolate-hazelnut spread on each triangle; from wider end, roll up pastry. Brush the egg on top of each roll.
3. Insert the drip tray into the bottom of the unit.
4. Spray the rolls with cooking spray and divide on the air racks. Place air racks into unit by sliding through the side grooves and onto the back lip.
5. Press the On/Off button, select Bake setting, set the temperature to 190ºC and the cooking time to 12 minutes. Press the On/Off button again to begin cooking, until pastry is golden brown.
6. When the cooking is complete, let the rolls cool on a wire rack. Serve while warm or at room temperature.

APPENDIX 1: BASIC KITCHEN CONVERSIONS & EQUIVALENTS

DRY MEASUREMENTS CONVERSION CHART

3 teaspoons = 1 tablespoon = 1/16 cup

6 teaspoons = 2 tablespoons = 1/8 cup

12 teaspoons = 4 tablespoons = ¼ cup

24 teaspoons = 8 tablespoons = ½ cup

36 teaspoons = 12 tablespoons = ¾ cup

48 teaspoons = 16 tablespoons = 1 cup

METRIC TO US COOKING CONVERSIONS

OVEN TEMPERATURES

120 °C = 250 °F

160 °C = 320 °F

180 °C = 350 °F

205 °C = 400 °F

220 °C = 425 °F

LIQUID MEASUREMENTS

CONVERSION CHART

8 fluid ounces = 1 cup = ½ pint = ¼ quart

16 fluid ounces = 2 cups = 1 pint = ½ quart

32 fluid ounces = 4 cups = 2 pints = 1 quart = ¼ gallon

128 fluid ounces = 16 cups = 8 pints = 4

quarts = 1 gallon

BAKING IN GRAMS

1 cup flour = 140 grams

1 cup sugar = 150 grams

1 cup powdered sugar = 160 grams

1 cup heavy cream = 235 grams

VOLUME

1 milliliter = 1/5 teaspoon

5 ml = 1 teaspoon

15 ml = 1 tablespoon

240 ml = 1 cup or 8 fluid ounces

1 liter = 34 fluid ounces

WEIGHT

1 gram = .035 ounces

100 grams = 3.5 ounces

500 grams = 1.1 pounds

1 kilogram = 35 ounces

US TO METRIC COOKING CONVERSIONS

1/5 tsp = 1 ml

1 tsp = 5 ml

1 tbsp = 15 ml

1 fluid ounces = 30 ml

1 cup = 237 ml

1 pint (2 cups) = 473 ml

1 quart (4 cups) = .95 liter

1 gallon (16 cups) = 3.8 liters

1 oz = 28 grams

1 pound = 454 grams

BUTTER

1 cup butter = 2 sticks = 8 ounces = 230 grams = 16 tablespoons

WHAT DOES 1 CUP EQUAL

1 cup = 8 fluid ounces

1 cup = 16 tablespoons

1 cup = 48 teaspoons

1 cup = ½ pint

1 cup = ¼ quart

1 cup = 1/16 gallon

1 cup = 240 ml

BAKING PAN CONVERSIONS

9-inch round cake pan = 12 cups

10-inch tube pan =16 cups

10-inch bundt pan = 12 cups

9-inch springform pan = 10 cups

9 x 5 inch loaf pan = 8 cups

9-inch square pan = 8 cups

BAKING PAN CONVERSIONS

1 cup all-purpose flour = 4.5 oz

1 cup rolled oats = 3 oz

1 large egg = 1.7 oz

1 cup butter = 8 oz

1 cup milk = 8 oz

1 cup heavy cream = 8.4 oz

1 cup granulated sugar = 7.1 oz

1 cup packed brown sugar = 7.75 oz

1 cup vegetable oil = 7.7 oz

1 cup unsifted powdered sugar = 4.4 oz

APPENDIX 2: RECIPES INDEX

Printed in Great Britain
by Amazon

37123177R00044